How to
Reach and Teach All
Students—Simplified

Elizabeth Breaux

EYE ON EDUCATION
6 DEPOT WAY WEST, SUITE 106
LARCHMONT, NY 10538
(914) 833–0551
(914) 833–0761 fax
www.eyeoneducation.com

Library of Congress Cataloging-in-Publication Data

Breaux, Elizabeth, 1961-
    How to reach and teach all students—simplified / Elizabeth Breaux.
        p. cm.
    ISBN 1-59667-042-8
    1. Teaching. 2. Effective teaching. 3. Motivation in education. I.
Title.
LB1025.3.B744 2006
371.1'02—dc22

                                                          2006030190

10 9 8 7 6 5 4 3 2 1

Editorial and production services provided by
Richard H. Adin Freelance Editorial Services
52 Oakwood Blvd., Poughkeepsie, NY 12603-4112
(845-471-3566)

Also Available from EYE ON EDUCATION

Dedication

This Book Is Dedicated to the Memories of
Elbi (1992–2006) and Gis (1988–2002),
for Without the Love of Puppies,
I Would Not Have Truly Lived.

Foreword

We cannot teach students until we reach them. We may possess numerous academic degrees, many years of experience, and a high IQ. We may employ the most effective lesson plans in a state-of-the-art facility with the most advanced technology. But these do not matter if we cannot first reach our students. Great teachers not only teach us well but also touch us on a human level—they reach into our inner depths and capture our hearts and souls, and they open our minds to all the knowledge they have to impart. They are the true teachers of the world. We thank them because we could not be who we are today had they not reached into our minds, touched our hearts, and imparted their infinite amounts of wisdom.

In my work in school districts across the country, I often see the same slogan used over and over: "Children First!" We plaster this across our hallways, our administrative offices, our school board offices, and our communities. Sometimes, however, we forget to put it in the most important places—our classrooms and our minds. When making decisions that affect our children, we must always consider first what is truly best for the children, not what is most comfortable or familiar to us. We chose this profession because we love children above all. We continue to choose this profession every day as we make life-changing decisions that will influence lives forever. Our influence never ends.

About the Author

Elizabeth Breaux is one of the most practical, down-to-earth, informative, and entertaining authors and speakers in education today. She has spoken to audiences across the country, leaving them laughing, crying, and certain that they have chosen the right profession—teaching. She is the author of two best-selling books: *Classroom Management Simplified* and *Real Teachers, Real Challenges, Real Solutions.*

A former curriculum coordinator and classroom teacher, she currently works with new teachers in the Lafayette Parish (Louisiana) School System. She is also one of the coordinators of TIPS, an induction program for new teachers in Lafayette. In addition, she trains assessors for the Louisiana Department of Education and travels as a national presenter for the Bureau of Education and Research.

Liz has taught and worked with at-risk students for 21 years, and she believes there is not a more challenging and rewarding job in the world. Her message has always been a simple one: "I cannot teach my students until I reach my students."

Table of Contents

Introduction

> *A child comes to me*
> *A soiled dove with heavy wings*
> *Flailing aimlessly*
> *Angry at everything and everyone*
> *At nothing and no one*
> *Rejected, ridiculed, misunderstood*
> *Hurting, injured, waiting to be healed*
> *I must first reach him and pull him in*
> *Before I can help him to fly again.*
>
> Elizabeth Breaux
> *Real Teachers, Real Challenges, Real Solutions*

What I've Learned About Teaching

- ◆ I've learned that teaching is hard work.
- ◆ I've learned that the job description is only the beginning of a teacher's responsibilities.
- ◆ I've learned that students are all different yet innately quite the same.
- ◆ I've learned that all students are reachable and teachable individuals.
- ◆ I've learned that students yearn for leaders (teachers) who are assertive.
- ◆ I've learned that students detest weakness in adults.
- ◆ I've learned that a calm, caring, and structured environment is necessary for human growth.
- ◆ I've learned that students respect authority if that authority is fair, kind, consistent, caring, and genuine.

◆ I've learned that the quality of the teacher is the determining factor in the success of the students.

How to Use This Book

This book will take you into the classrooms of many teachers who face the same challenges that all of today's teachers must conquer. In each chapter, a typical situation will be given, along with sections on what works and what doesn't work, culminating in a chapter summary.

In Part I, you will find nine chapters on how to *reach* students, followed by five chapters in Part II on how to *teach* students. As you read through each chapter, you will undoubtedly be reminded of the actions of your former teachers, your fellow teachers, and yourself. My wish is that you will feel validated, self-assured, and eager to take additional steps to become a better teacher with each passing day and year. Always remember, "Children First!"

What This Book Will Do for You

- ◆ If you want to truly make a difference in the lives of all students
- ◆ If you want to have the power to be a leader in the classroom
- ◆ If you want to reach each student so that you can teach each student
- ◆ If you want to create a calm, caring, and structured environment
- ◆ If you want to be the determining factor in the success of your students

…then this book is the one for you!

How to Reach
All Students

Of Puppies and of People

He's just a little puppy, so care for him I must
I can see it in his eyes; he's giving me his trust
And that is not an easy thing, for he has been abused
Abandoned and neglected, battered, scorned, and used
I scoop him up into my arms, he shivers and he stares
He's hoping that this new one is the one whose life he'll share
I know I cannot let him down; I am his final straw
His one last chance for happiness, compassion, love, and awe
I think about that puppy now and the years he shared my home
From the moment I reached out to him his days alone were gone
So I pray that I can hold each child like that puppy to my heart
And make them know that in this world they truly are a part
I'll give them confidence and pride and eagerness to grow
I'll reach them then I'll teach them and the right path I will show
For in my hands I hold the key that opens up a world
Of endless possibilities to every boy and girl
So help me, Lord, to not forget that you've given me the power
To change the world inside these walls each second, minute, hour
And to know there is no schoolhouse grand—no chapel, shrine, nor steeple
That means a thing without the love of puppies and of people…

Elizabeth Breaux

I Am the Student

You are the adult and I am the student
A vital distinction requiring your prudence
So mean what you say, and say what you mean
Do unto me, and I'll do the same
For I am in tune to your every move
Your actions, reactions, and your attitude
Tell me I'm good and good I will be
Expect my best, and my best you will see
Be nice and inviting and I will come in
Look into my eyes and I'll raise my chin
Be firm, yet kind, and I will respond
Give me a choice and I'll choose the right one
Tell me I'm better than I've ever been
And I'll rise to the challenge and hurdle the fence
But please don't give up, when I fall to the ground
Just help me back up and I'll quickly rebound.

Elizabeth Breaux

First Impressions: Getting Students on Your Side

Think about your all-time favorite teacher. Think about your all-time least favorite teacher. Chances are, you remember both with a similar amount of clarity. Good or bad, they both made an impression on you. Positive or negative, the impression was lasting. You may not have realized it at the time, but you knew on the very first day of school whether you really liked the teacher or whether the year would be a long one.

The impression that you make on the first day of school is critical. The students are sizing you up from the moment they meet you. They are watching you like a clock, and they are making mental notes of your every move, action, and reaction.

The initial impression you make on your students on the first day of school will set the tone for the remainder of the year. It is a foundation that is as critical as the one on which the school building itself rests. "But what if I'm reading this in October, or January, or April?" you ask. "Do I have to wait until the start of the next school year to make some necessary changes?" The answer to that question, of course, is a resounding *no!* That's what is so great about teaching. In my work with teachers who are new to the profession, I often tell them exactly this: "You can have a 'Monday' whenever you choose!" Optimally, however, we want to lay our foundations on the first day(s) of school and then build on that foundation throughout the school year. If the foundation is properly laid, we won't have to go through a re-building phase throughout the year. However, we do have the option of going back to fix cracks in the foundation if necessary. The bottom line is this: Do it right the first time, and your focus can remain fixed on the building phase. Keep your eyes wide open for cracks, however, and fix them immediately before the building begins to crumble!

Think about one of your first days of school as a student. What were you looking for or hoping for from your teachers? What is it that you are still looking for or hoping for when you receive instruction from a college professor, principal, supervisor, mentor, or any staff development presenter? Are those the same qualities that your students find in you?

A few years ago, I surveyed a group of sixth-grade students at a local middle school. I asked them to think about their favorite teacher (this was a "teaming" school, and all of the students had five different teachers that year). I asked them to tell me one thing about their favorite teacher (without giving the name of the teacher). I was familiar with the school and its teachers, so the results were very interesting to me. I knew exactly which teachers they were talking about in their descriptions. Here are some of the results:

- "She is very nice to all of us."
- "My teacher takes care of us and says we are like her own children."
- "My teacher is happy that she is a teacher and likes her job."
- "I think he likes me a lot. He always helps me and the others, too."
- "In some classes I am so bad, but I never get in trouble in her class."

- "She makes us work a lot and she helps us a lot, but I don't mind because I get mostly As."
- "He is funny and interesting."
- "Sometimes I look at the clock and the class is over and I think it just started."
- "She never screams or fusses at us because we are all good in there."
- "It makes me want to do good when I walk in there."
- "We do lots of fun things in there that is work and for a grade but it's still fun."
- "She sends my momma a note when I do good and it's on the refrigerator."

Imagine that the students in your class are asked to describe you. Which of these descriptions might they use to characterize you?

Situation

 It's the first day of school and the morning bell rings. The students at this alternative school have been placed here because of poor behavior that has resulted in either excessive suspensions or expulsion from their assigned schools. Most enter with trepidation because of their perceived expectations. Because they are all the "victims" of someone else's decisions, few take responsibility for their actions. Obviously, none are excited about being here. This is *not* a happy day.

Ms. You and Ms. Me both began teaching here at the same time, 15 years ago. Both are experienced with these types of students. Both have built reputations for themselves. The principal at this school can tell you without reserve that he or she rarely has to deal with any discipline problems stemming from Ms. You's classroom. He will also tell you that the bulk of the school's discipline referrals for the year will most likely come from Ms. Me.

What Works

 Ms. You stands at the door, greeting each student with her usual inviting smile, jovial tone, handshake, and pat on the back. As the students enter the room, they are overwhelmed by the welcoming environment. Welcome signs surround the room. Gift bags are on the desks awaiting each student. Ms. You pulls her chair and places it right in the middle of the aisle so that she is centered among the students. She studies the 20 pairs of eyes, seemingly looking right through each pair. When she is certain that she has their attention, she says, "If I were to share with you the details of some of the things that I did when I was younger, there would be a few things that I would be ashamed to share. I won't do that, but the point is that we have all done things that we are not so proud of having done. You are here because you have made some mistakes, but those mistakes are in the past, as much as mine are in my past. We don't need to talk about them. We need only to remember them so that they can serve as constant reminders of what we don't ever want to do again. I don't really care about what brought you here. I care only about what we do from this day forward. That's all that really matters in the long run anyway."

Ms. You has obviously gotten their attention, so she takes advantage of their attentive minds and begins one of her favorite opening-day activities: "I am going to give you 15 seconds to check out the room and to find as many *brown* items as you possibly can. At the end of the 15 seconds, I will ask you to lower your head and make a list of at least 10 brown items that you located. You will have to keep your eyes on your paper, because the goal will be to write down only what you can remember from the 15 seconds that you spent searching." (An observer would notice that the students are already scanning the room.)

"OK," says Ms. You, "Ready, set, go!" The students frantically search every nook of the room, from ceiling to floor, while Ms. You chants "brown, brown, find brown, find brown items!" Fifteen seconds expire, and Ms. You stops the students. "Lower your head, with eyes looking only at your paper, and don't look up. You will rely only on your memory as you make a list of at least 10 *green* items!" Moans and grumbles can be heard from all. "Green?" asks one student. "Yes, and keep your eyes on your paper," says Ms. You. "I only want green...as many green items as you can remember."

After a few seconds, Ms. You stops the students and tells them that they can look up. "What's the matter?" asks Ms. You. "You said to look for brown items," answer the students. "Oh, that's right, I did say that. How many of you could have listed at least ten *brown* items?" (All of the students raise their hands.) "How many of you were having trouble listing the 10 *green* items?" (All raise their hands!) "Can someone tell me why you were having so much trouble? I'm noticing now as I look around the room that there are far more green items than brown items in this room," explains Ms. You. "You told us to look for brown, so that's what we did. We weren't looking for green," explains one student, as others agree.

"So," says Ms. You, "It seems that you are all telling me that because you were focusing on brown, you found only brown items. You were not focused on green, so your mind was completely oblivious to all of the green items around you!" "Oh, I see," says a student. "We can't learn one thing if we are focusing on something else." "That's right," says Ms. You. Mission accomplished!

Ms. You sits back in her chair, looks again at each of those 20 pairs of attentive eyes, and says, "Again, what we focus on from this day forward is all that matters. We cannot lose our focus, or we will lose sight of what is important. We cannot forget our past because if we do, we will fail to learn from our mistakes. We will use those past mistakes, however, to help us focus on a better future—beginning today."

What Doesn't Work

 Just down the hallway, another class enters Ms. Me's room. Ms. Me is waiting at her doorway, but the greeting is less than jovial. In fact, Ms. Me is talking to the teacher across the hall, and she doesn't seem to notice the students entering her room. There is no "Welcome" or "Good morning" or "Glad to see you" here. Ms. Me slams the door—a tactic that she uses every day to show the students at the outset just who is in charge of her classroom. Ms. Me then completes her second task (tactic), forcefully placing a stack of discipline referrals on the front of her desk, where they serve as a constant threat to the students.

Ms. Me hands out the textbooks and tells the students to open them to page 1 and begin reading. (How else will the class finish the book if they waste time on frivolous opening-day activities?) Each student reluctantly follows her directions—a few actually begin reading, but the rest do a really good job of pretending.

Summary

 Both teachers have made an indelible first impression. There is no doubt that each student knows what to expect from each teacher for the remainder of the school year. Tomorrow, their minds will open as they enter Ms. You's room. Her students will be eager to uncover the surprises that they already know await them in Ms. You's room. You see, in her wisdom, Ms. You knows that she has to first make a great first impression in order to infuse her students with high expectations (which she must continue to meet). This won't be easy, but she knows that the only way to teach students is to reach them first.

The students also know exactly what to expect from their next visit to Ms. Me's classroom. They will miraculously transform their attitudes and demeanors when they enter. Their minds will involuntarily close, and their self-discipline (which they have already begun to display in Ms. You's room)

will cease to exist. Their eager young minds will transform into ones that have little confidence or expectations. There will be no surprises in Ms. Me's room either, other than the ones the students bring each day—the ones that will cost them many trips to the office or possibly some other facility.

No Harmful Words Allowed

I've finally come to realize that my attitude's infectious
It permeates my classroom, it calms and it protects us
It causes some to wonder what goes on behind my door
And wish that they could teach my kids (not the ones that they abhor)
They watch the transformation as the children walk inside
But don't dare to ask my "secret," for that might scar their pride
My "secret" is quite simple, "harmful words are not allowed!
I simply find the good in all, and then shout it, shout it loud!"

Elizabeth Breaux

The Power of Thanks and Praise: Accentuating the Positive

Think about how good you feel when someone compliments you on a job well done. It feels good, doesn't it? In fact, thanks and praise are addictive. They are the drugs that keep us yearning for more of the great feelings that they elicit—the more we get, the more we want and need!

It has been proven over and over again that positive people are much more likely to get what they want in life. Positive people are more likely to attain their goals. Positive people attract other positive people because it simply feels good to be around people who spread good feelings. Good things just seem to happen to people who can maintain a positive outlook about their future. But the truth is, not much in this life just happens. We create our destinies through our mind-set and our actions.

Nowhere is this more obvious than in the classroom. Positive teachers seem to breed positive students. Students' attitudes and behaviors will eventually mimic those of the teacher—good or bad, positive or negative. If you truly believe this, you will come to affirm that you have the power to make a difference in your classroom through your attitude and behaviors.

Unfortunately, we teachers have become skilled at spotting negatives. We seem to know that they are coming before they arrive. We await them! We have gestures, comments, and consequences ready to spew at a moment's notice. What we often fail to notice or acknowledge is that positive things are occurring in our classrooms at any given time. If we could simply train ourselves to become more astute at spotting the positives (as opposed to spotting the negatives), we could completely turn around the climate of our classrooms. We truly have that power!

Situation

 It's the first day of school at Rees Middle School, an inner-city school with a high-poverty student body. Challenges are abundant, the failure rate is high, and teacher morale is low. We will look into the classrooms of two teachers, Mrs. Upbeat and Mrs. Downbeat. Both teach the seventh grade, and both are veteran teachers. Mrs. Upbeat views challenges as a chance to grow. Mrs. Downbeat believes that she has been victimized by her students, administrators, parents, and society, and therefore she has completely relinquished her power.

Again, same school, same students, same grade level...but *different* teacher attitudes and very different results.

What Works

 The morning bell rings, and the students "somewhat eagerly" shuffle to their first period classes. (It's the first day of school; therefore, there is some degree of excitement and anticipation.) Mrs. Upbeat waits in her doorway, ready to welcome each student on this important first day.

Because Mrs. Upbeat has learned that positive attitudes breed more positive attitudes, she is ready to begin planting the seeds immediately. The tardy bell rings. Mrs. Upbeat closes the door, faces her students, and says, "My goodness! In all of my years of teaching I have never seen a class walk in so quietly and be seated so promptly! This must be my lucky year! Thank you, thank you, thank you!" What Mrs. Upbeat has just so ingeniously done is to ensure this behavior will be repeated yet again tomorrow. When the students enter the room tomorrow, they will remember the thanks and praise they received the day before, and they will do it again. They have already learned that this is the type of behavior that is expected—and rewarded—in this classroom.

In her many years of teaching, Mrs. Upbeat has learned that there are certain positive behaviors that are ongoing, and in order to keep them ongoing, we must continue to thank, compliment, and praise our students. Too often, we view certain behaviors as expected, and therefore, we don't bother to let students know how much we appreciate them. Mrs. Upbeat knows that she must continue to thank and praise her students for any and all positive behaviors if she wants the behaviors to continue.

On the first day of school, an observer would notice that Mrs. Upbeat thanks and praises her students for such trivial things as

- Walking into the room quietly
- Giving her their attention
- Raising their hands to speak
- Bringing materials
- Doing their work
- Picking up trash before leaving
- Walking quietly to lunch

But what if the students are *not* already doing these things? Mrs. Upbeat has a trick for getting students to do exactly what she wants. How does she do this? She thanks them *before* the behavior ever occurs. That's right! If Mrs. Upbeat sees a piece of trash on the floor, she thanks a nearby student for picking it up for her, and they just do it. Before class even began the first day, she thanked the students in advance for raising their hands to speak (even though none had spoken yet), saying that she just "can't hear when everyone is speaking at once."

Mrs. Upbeat has even become a master at giving criticism in a positive and praising way. "Oh, I just love that idea you have for the topic of your paragraph. As soon as you get those details in correct order, however, it will be just awesome. May I suggest that you use this detail first, and then build on that? And *please* let me see it as soon as you finish. I can't wait to read it!"

Mrs. Upbeat knows that even a negative situation can be dealt with in a positive way. She has bought in to the thinking that there are no bad kids, just bad decisions. Mrs. Upbeat knows that we must never attack the child, just the bad decision.

Mrs. Upbeat also knows that this attitude of hers cannot flicker or wane. It must remain embedded in the day-to-day classroom setting in order for her and her students to be happy, positive, and ultimately successful.

> ## Thank Me
>
> *My teacher says "Thank you" for everything*
> *For things you just wouldn't believe*
> *So, teachers, I'm sending a message to you*
> *One I hope that you will retrieve.*
>
> *If you thank me for the little things*
> *Where "thank yous" are not expected*
> *Then the bad things (that I sometimes do)*
> *Will soon be redirected.*
>
> *Some of us need you to notice us*
> *Whether for good or for bad*
> *And it seems the bad kids get your attention*
> *That they otherwise wouldn't have.*
>
> *So thank me for smiling and walking in line*
> *Thank me for listening and being on time*
> *Thank me for doing my work and you'll see*
> *That I'll be the best kid, for you, I can be!*
>
>
>
> Elizabeth Breaux
> *Classroom Management Simplified*
>
>

What Doesn't Work

 Mrs. Downbeat's students, although they don't know it yet, will literally be beaten down from the minute they arrive in class. "Don't you even think about walking in my room with your shirt hanging out of your pants," she says to one student. "And if anyone else in here thinks they are going to come in looking like this, they are certainly mistaken," she bellows. She has managed to agitate (and lose) several students before the first bell of the new school year has rung. Mrs. Downbeat failed to notice that the other 20 students were dressed to code, so she missed a perfect opportunity to praise those who did it right! By the way, in most cases, if we simply praise those who are in compliance, those who are not will see what is expected and eventually come on board. Mrs. Downbeat could have asked that everyone check themselves to make certain their shirts were tucked in and then thanked them all for being so cooperative.

The bell rings and Mrs. Downbeat immediately lays down the law:

- "If you think you're going to talk in this class, you've got another thought coming!" (I've still not figured out what "another thought" is.)
- "A few of you are in here for the second time. I hope you've learned your lesson. And don't think you're going to get away with anything this year!"
- "Detention starts today, for any of you who are interested."

Amazingly—and understandably—in the first few minutes of class, Mrs. Downbeat has managed to draw out attitudes in her students that mirror her own. Several students have already begun to engage in the most detested of all disrespectful behaviors:

- Sucking teeth
- Eye rolling
- Pencil tapping
- Humming
- Ripping out and wadding up notebook paper
- Turning sideways in their desks
- Refusing to work
- Pretending to have sudden hearing loss
- Walking away

Do any of these behaviors look or sound familiar? Mrs. Downbeat has already managed to alienate her students on the very first day of school. I'll spare you the agony of the rest of the details of a day—or worse, a year—in Mrs. Downbeat's classroom. Suffice it to say that Mrs. Downbeat doesn't do a lot of thanking and praising this year (or any year). She doesn't believe in thanking students for doing something they are already expected to do. More lost opportunities…

Summary

 The teacher's choice is simply to *choose* to accentuate the positives or magnify the negatives. If you want a positive classroom environment in which students are eager to please because they know that their good acts and works will be validated, then start accentuating the positives—not just some of the time, but *all of the time*. If accentuating the positives doesn't feel natural to you, then practice. Really, there's nothing wrong with that. Literally make a list of all of the positive things that go on daily in your classroom. Your list might look something like this:

- Brought materials to class
- Turned in homework
- Completed work
- Worked well in groups
- Raised hands to speak
- Picked up trash
- Volunteered to participate
- Helped someone else
- Said "thank you" or "excuse me" or "I'm sorry"
- Volunteered to help the teacher
- Passed out papers
- Wrote a nice topic sentence (if the rest is awful, compliment the student on what's good first, then he or she will be willing to listen to what needs work)

CAUTION: Be genuine! Students see insincerities coming from a mile away. Contrary to popular belief, they are not easy to fool. Never praise a job that is not well done just because you want to shower students with praise. Find the good—the real good—and compliment that, but don't neglect to fix what needs fixing!

Lost Within a Shout

You yelled at me and I yelled back
What else was there to do?
We yelled some more, our throats got sore
And the tension grew and grew
And finally, in exhaustion, we both ran out of steam
Left standing in embarrassment, no pride left to redeem
What point is there in thinking, that to be "right" we must
Keep pushing on till all involved just lose respect and trust?
Maybe if we'd listened, we could have met half way
Let's talk next time and really hear what the other has to say
For if we both could do that, maybe we'd find out
That never has a point been made when lost within a shout!

Annette Breaux
Real Teachers, Real Challenges, Real Solutions

The Assertive and In-Control Teacher: Taking Control of Your Classroom

First, let's make certain we all understand that there is a huge difference between being *controlling* and being *in-control*!

People who are assertive and in control are self-confident and forceful, although not in a controlling way. Assertive people usually have little trouble maintaining control of situations while not losing the respect of those involved. Assertive people are never demeaning, loud, bossy, or arrogant, yet they are always in control.

Controlling people, on the other hand, are scheming, calculating, and aggressive (i.e., violent, hostile, destructive, belligerent). Controlling people usually lose control of themselves under the guise of trying to control others. In other words, to control others, controlling people first model how to lose control of themselves.

We all have much experience with both types. The following are characteristics of teachers who are in control and assertive and of teachers who are controlling by nature.

Teachers who are in control and assertive

- Would never dream of getting into a power struggle with a student
- Treat students with the utmost respect and expect the same in return
- Are consistent in the implementation of rules and procedures (see Chapters 4 and 5)
- Would never embarrass a student, especially in front of his or her peers
- Realize that dislike erects a barrier between the teacher and the student, making any exchange of knowledge virtually impossible
- Never raise their voices in anger to a student
- Are firm yet kind
- Have high expectations and a zero-tolerance policy for unacceptable behavior (the penalty or consequence, however, always fits the crime, and implementation is consistent)
- Realize that they are constantly modeling the behavior that they expect from their students, and so they always behave accordingly
- Are masters at spotting the positives and bringing them to the forefront
- Use administration as a last resort or backup for themselves as the prime disciplinarian and classroom manager

On the other hand, controlling teachers

- Often get into power struggles with students
- Are disrespectful of students and disrespected by students
- Use embarrassment as a way of dealing with students
- Are often inconsistent in the implementation of rules and procedures, causing students to view them as unfair
- Don't care whether students like them or their class

- Seldom make positive home contacts
- Tend to believe they are victims of students
- Often scream at students
- Have a serious dislike for those who are in control
- Are masters at spotting the negatives
- Use office referrals as scare tactics and often count on the administration to make students behave appropriately

It is truly a choice. Do you or do you not want to be the adult, in control of your own classroom? If the answer is yes—and of course it is—then you must realize that you have the power. First, evaluate yourself using the foregoing lists. Which qualities characterize you the most?

The following situation looks into the classrooms of two teachers who are attending a staff development session. That's right—they're absent from school! Therefore, we will be looking at a typical day in the lives of two substitute teachers who are in the classroom in the absence of the regular teachers. For those of you who have taught long enough to have needed someone to take your place, you realize just how important a good substitute teacher can be. Although we realize that no one can *really* take our place, we hope that at the very least, we will find someone who can maintain control. We realize that our little angels are capable of losing their wings if given the opportunity—and we don't want anyone to come into our rooms who will give them that opportunity!

I remember how important it was to me that I find a substitute who had many of the qualities of an assertive and in-control teacher whenever I knew that I was going to be away from school. I remember that I once canceled a planned trip because the substitute who had been hired to replace me was known for having every single quality from the "controlling teacher" list, and I simply refused to do that to my students!

Situation

 Today is a staff development day for all fifth-grade teachers at I. M. N. Control Elementary School. Substitute teachers have been hired for the five fifth-grade teachers. All fifth graders have been made aware that will be happening, so there are no surprises other than the substitute assignments for each classroom.

We will look into two classrooms in which the students are (usually) extremely well behaved, and effective instruction and a healthy learning environment are the norm. We all know, however, that even the best students are capable of a complete metamorphosis when they are placed in the hands of another adult (a teacher or a substitute). We also know that finding five substitute teachers on any given day is a daunting task. Finding five substitute teachers (for one day) who are capable of coming in and maintaining control of their classrooms is almost impossible, even at I. M. N. Control Elementary School!

The teachers have prepared the students for this day, and they have left a sufficient amount of work for the students to complete. We will look in on the classrooms of two highly effective, highly efficient, and highly respected teachers.

What Works

 Mr. In-Control arrives early in the morning to familiarize himself with the lesson and to make certain that all necessary materials and supplies are ready for the students. He also locates the student roster and places it in a spot where it will be easily accessible. He notices that the teacher has left a seating chart, so he places that on the desk where it will be readily available also.

The regular classroom teacher has left her rules and procedures handbook on her desk, so Mr. In-Control uses the remaining 30 minutes before the morning bell to familiarize himself with it. About 10 minutes before the morning bell rings, Mr. In-Control walks to the auditorium, where he will meet his fifth-grade class. (According to the handbook, the students will be seated in Section 12.)

Mr. In-Control walks to section 12, where all eyes are on him—remember, they know that they will have a substitute teacher today—and he notices that about half the class is not yet seated. "Good morning," he blurts, in his jovial tone. "What a fine class you are! At least half of you are already seated and waiting for me, and I can tell that the rest of you were just about to take your seats!" (An observer would notice that the standers almost immediately become sitters.) "First," says Mr. In-Control, "Let's go ahead and walk in your usual line (I understand that you line up according to classroom rows) and we'll walk quietly to the room. Once we get there and you are all seated in the usual 10 seconds or less, I will introduce myself and tell you what we are going to do today. And one more thing: I can already tell that this is a great class and that we are going to have a wonderful day. Thank you in advance for all of the help that I know you are going to give me. Now, without any talking, let's line up and walk to class."

Because Mr. In-Control read the handbook in advance, he knows that the students are always given 10 seconds (after entering the room) to be at their own desks and seated. Mr. In-Control also knows that had he not let them know that he was already aware of the 10-second rule, the students may have "forgotten" to abide by it. He knows that just getting them to sit in the auditorium could have been a chore had he not used his assertive tactics—the same ones he used to get them to walk quietly to the classroom and find their seats (the assigned ones) within 10 seconds of entering.

The remainder of the class day is much the same: lots of sharing of teacher expectations, immediate follow-through, compliments, and thank yous. Not one student is sent to the office. All work is complete, and all students are happy. Mr. In-Control is able to shower them with even more praise at the end of the day.

When the regular classroom teacher returns the following day, she finds her room in order, exactly as she left it. All of the student work has been completed and placed neatly on her desk for her review. A lovely thank you note has been placed on her chair, thanking her for the privilege of spending a day with this wonderful group of fifth-graders, a note that she giddily reads to the students before beginning class.

What Doesn't Work

 The morning bell rings, and Mr. Lose-It wonders why there are no students in his classroom. (Mr. Lose-It has not bothered to arrive early to familiarize himself with the procedures.) He walks into the hallway and notices that the other teachers are leading their classes down the hallway and into their classrooms. He questions a neighboring teacher and learns that his class is awaiting him in the auditorium.

Mr. Lose-It is furious. "Someone could have told me that," he grumbles as he rushes down the hallway. (It is quite obvious to those watching that Mr. Lose-It is already having a bad day. His self-control is waning far too early.)

Mr. Lose-It "greets" his class—who are standing, talking, and having a pretty darn good time—with his "I am the one in control" voice: "Get over here right now and line up! Don't you think for one minute that you're going to behave like this with me today. I hope you've had fun, because it's the last fun you'll have today!"

The students glare at him, roll their eyes, suck their teeth, and finally line up. They already know the kind of day that they are going to have. "Why didn't you just walk with the others to your classroom? You do it every day." Several students test him as they are walking to class by defying his order to "Be quiet!" "You don't have to yell at us," screams one student. "We're right here—we can hear you!" "If you can hear me," snarls Mr. Lose-It, "then stop talking!" "You see," says another student, "You *are* yelling." "I'll show you what yelling is, young man. This is whispering compared to what I'll do if you don't stop with the comments right now!"

The students enter the classroom, and Mr. Lose-It barks at them to "Sit down and shut up. Your teacher left plenty of work for you to do. I don't want to hear any talking. None!" Mr. Lose-It then performs the controlling teacher's favorite maneuver: slamming a large stack of discipline referrals on the front of the teacher's desk, where they are in clear view of everyone and easily accessible to him. The large stack is fairly slim by the end of the day…

Summary

 In the classroom, as in life, we have no control over other people. We do, however, have total control over ourselves. It is only when we are in control of ourselves that others will take our lead and gain control of themselves. When that happens, we simply seem to be in control of others. That's the beauty of the whole thing: We often hear about teachers who are complimented by administrators and colleagues for being so in control of their classes. The reality is that they are in control of themselves, and they are modeling it in such a way that the students play "follow the leader" without even realizing it. *The truth is that we influence self-control in others by maintaining control of ourselves.*

Mr. In-Control obviously played that game by the book: He never lost control of himself.

- He did not allow power struggles to take place.
- He treated students with the utmost respect and got the same in return.
- He was consistent with the established rules and procedures.
- He did not embarrass any student.
- He made himself likeable to the students beginning with their first meeting, when he greeted them with a hearty "Good morning" and a "What a fine class of students you are!"
- He never raised his voice to the students.
- He was firm yet kind.
- He maintained the same zero-tolerance policy that had been established by the school.
- He was a perfect role model for his students.
- He began spotting the positives early that morning.
- He did not have to use the administration, but he did know that it was there as a last resort.

Mr. In-Control was in high demand for the remainder of that school year, with requests coming from both the teachers and the students. Mr. Lose-It, on the other hand, gained a reputation as the epitome of a controlling person. If you look back at the lists from the beginning of this chapter, you'll see that he fits the profile perfectly.

- He immediately got into a power struggle with a student.
- He was disrespectful of students, and they, in turn, were disrespectful of him.
- He did not follow the school's rules and procedures from the very beginning, and thus he got into a bind. He then unfairly blamed the students for his own mistake!
- He obviously did not care whether he established a good rapport with the students.
- He screamed at students throughout the day.
- He never took the opportunity to praise the students for the good things they did. For example, because he was the one who had messed up early in the morning, he could have taken the opportunity to praise them for remaining in the auditorium and waiting for him instead of chastising them for having the audacity to be standing and talking!
- He used office referrals as a scare tactic, which obviously didn't scare any of them, considering the number of students who were actually sent to the office that day.

To repeat: We cannot control others. We can control ourselves, however. To be in control of our classrooms, we must be models of self-control. Do that, and others will marvel at how in control you are of your classroom.

> **Help Me, Please!**
>
> *Walk inside and quiet down*
> *Take the book sacks off the ground*
> *Stay in your desk, why are you standing*
> *(I'm tired of all this reprimanding)*
> *A million times I know I've said it*
> *So how much longer till they get it*
> *Over and over the same old rhyme*
> *Once more and I'll lose my mind*
> *Why is it that they just don't listen*
> *And what is it that I am missing*
> *I've been nice and I've been mean*
> *I've spoken softly and I've screamed*
> *What more, I ask, is there to do*
> *Help me, please, I've not a clue!*
>
> Elizabeth Breaux

Implementing Procedures to Perfection: Three Simple Steps

Why is it that some teachers seem to get all the good kids every year? You know the ones:

- Their students always walk in straight lines.
- The bell rings and they are all seated and ready for the day.
- They raise their hands to ask a question.
- They raise their hands to ask permission to leave their desks.
- The teacher tells them to get into their groups, and they move with diligence and purpose.

- The teacher asks for their attention, and all are immediately attentive.
- They turn in their homework.
- They get good grades.
- They clean their spaces before leaving class.
- They wait for permission to leave the class once the bell has rung.
- They leave class in an orderly manner.

Stop trying to wake yourself—you're not dreaming! This really is the norm in many classrooms, and it is not because all of the students just happen to be perfect angels. The truth is, if you were to watch every one of these students as they leave this room and enter another, you would likely find that several of them would not be doing any of these things in other classrooms. So what is going on?

An observer in one of these classrooms may not have a clue as to why things are running so beautifully because all of the work has already been done. You see, the teachers in these classrooms know that they must spend the first few days of the school year teaching their students all of the procedures they expect them to follow for the rest of the year. These procedures are then practiced and become routine. An observer wouldn't see all of the hard work that has gone into this—he or she would just see a classroom that is running efficiently and effectively. The best part of all is that the teacher is having fun teaching, and the students are pretty darn happy, too!

Before we go on about procedures, let's first determine the difference between a rule and a procedure:

- A *rule* has a consequence attached to it. Students receive a punishment or a consequence if a rule is broken. (We'll talk more specifically about rules in Chapter 5.)

- A *procedure* is a day-to-day classroom function that makes the lesson run smoothly. There is no need to implement a consequence or a punishment if a procedure is not performed correctly because no rule has been violated. (Exception: A child who willfully refuses to follow a procedure after adequate practice time may need a consequence. Before doing so, however, exhaust all other possibilities, such as calling the parent or having a one-on-one conversation with the student.)

A well-managed classroom will have many procedures and just a few rules. If the teacher implements the procedures effectively, many of what we used to consider rules can become procedures.

Three critical steps are necessary to implement procedures to perfection:

1. Teach

2. Practice

3. Implement

In step one, the *teaching* step, the teacher must literally teach the students exactly how a particular procedure is to be done. Tell them, show them, and then tell them again and show them again.

In step two, the *practicing* step, the teacher must allow the students to try the procedure themselves. This can be great fun and a wonderful learning experience. Tell your students that this is the time to mess up! In fact, encourage them to make mistakes. Tell them it's alright to make mistakes in order to learn the proper way. (This is great psychology because you can take away the students' temptation to do it incorrectly simply to aggravate the teacher.)

In step three, the *implementation* step, the teacher begins the *consistent* implementation of what has been taught and practiced. If a student performs the procedure incorrectly, the teacher simply reminds him or her of the correct procedure and then practices it until it becomes routine.

Note: Notice the key word—consistent. Consistency is the key. The teacher must remain consistent in his or her actions, or students will not take the procedures seriously. I have seen many classrooms in which teachers' good intentions have fallen prey to a failure to be consistent in the implementation phase. Therefore, it is critical for the teacher to stop any actions that are inconsistent with the correct implementation of a procedure; otherwise, the incorrect implementation is the one that will become the routine or procedure.

Students want structure and consistency. Without them, there can be no building of trust. Unfortunately, these qualities are often lacking in the classrooms of teachers who seem to get all of the "bad kids" every year.

Situation

It is the first day of school, and Teachers A and B are anxiously awaiting the arrival of their fifth-graders. These two teachers are considered a team in that they teach the same two groups of students. They each teach one group in the morning and one in the afternoon.

Teacher A has accrued many years of teaching experience and is no novice when it comes to setting procedures on the first day of school. Teacher B is a first-year teacher and has not yet learned the ropes. Let's make it perfectly clear, however, that both of the teachers have many of the same qualities:

◆ They love teaching.

◆ They love students.

◆ They are highly knowledgeable in their content area.

◆ They are highly qualified to teach in their content area.

◆ They are organized.

◆ They are very personable and likeable.

◆ They have created an inviting learning environment in their classroom.

There is, however, one very distinct difference—a difference that will make these two classrooms look as though they are polar opposites. Obviously, it is not because one teacher got all the good kids and one got all the bad kids. They are teaching the same students!

What Works

Students enter Teacher A's classroom in a semi-orderly manner (as most do on the first day of school). Teacher A thanks them profusely for doing so, and then she proceeds to explain the "correct" procedure that will be used from now on when they come to her classroom.

"That was very nice," Teacher A says to the students. "Beginning tomorrow, however, we will use a different procedure for coming to class in the morning. I have morning duty in the cafeteria, so I will designate an area where we will meet. When the morning bell rings, we will meet in the designated area and then walk together to class. Right now, I would like us to go to the cafeteria so that I can show you the designated area. We will pretend that it is another day, and we'll practice doing it the right way. Oh, and because we are going to leave here right now, we can also practice the procedure that we will use when going to lunch each day! Here's what I expect you to do. When lunchtime arrives, we will line up in the room and walk quietly to the cafeteria without talking. (There will be other classes in progress, and we don't want to disturb them.) Of course you may talk, using your inside voices, once we are in the cafeteria each day. OK, let's try it! Remember, we will first practice walking quietly to the cafeteria, and once we're there, we'll practice walking from the cafeteria to class, as we will do each morning."

Teacher A reminds the students that once they have lined up and moved outside the classroom, there is to be no talking. The students line up, and Teacher A leads them out of the classroom. They begin their quiet journey to the cafeteria. Teacher A thanks them for the beautiful job they are doing. An observer would notice that Teacher A keeps her finger to her lips (the quiet gesture) as a constant reminder. The students arrive in the cafeteria, and Teacher A says to them, " OK, that was awesome—now you can talk!" (Silence. Isn't it funny how students suddenly lose the use of their vocal cords when they are asked to talk?)

Teacher A tells the students that she would now like to practice the procedure for coming to class each morning. (She takes the students to a designated area in the back of the cafeteria, where there are several tables that are not used at breakfast time.) "Once you finish eating your breakfast each morning, you are to come directly to these tables, where you will sit and wait for the bell to ring. You will not leave this area until I arrive. You may talk, read, or complete your homework assignment while you wait for me. Now, I want all of you to have a seat here at these tables."

All of the students sit, and Teacher A walks to the front of the cafeteria. Once she gets there, she tells them that this is her duty station. When the morning bell rings, she will come to meet them. (Teacher A wants them to know that she can see them clearly from her duty station.)

"Now, let's pretend that the bell has just rung. What should you do?" Several students answer, "Wait for you!" "Oops! I forgot to tell you something," says Teacher A. "I can't understand you unless you raise your hand!" Several hands go up, and Teacher A calls on one student. "We should wait for you," says the student. "That's right," says Teacher A. "I understood you perfectly that time! Thanks for raising your hand. That's another procedure we'll talk about once we get back to class, but I think you already understand it just fine! Now let's line up and walk quietly to class. And remember, no talking now because other students are already in class."

Teacher A leads the students back to the classroom. (Again, Teacher A showers them with praise on the way back to class. She knows this will ensure that the behavior will continue.) Once they get to the doorway, she stops them, thanks them emphatically for following the procedure so precisely, and then tells them that once they enter the classroom, they are to go directly to their desks, be seated, and await her instruction. Once the students do this, she reviews the procedures that she has just taught.

Teacher A has just *taught* and *practiced* the following five procedures:

+ Meeting the teacher in the morning
+ Walking quietly in line to the classroom each morning
+ Entering the classroom each morning
+ Exiting the classroom and walking quietly to lunch
+ Raising hands to speak

Now, she can begin the *consistent* implementation of these procedures immediately. And by the way, she hopes that some students actually fail to follow the procedures correctly on the first day: That will give her an opportunity to thank all of the students who do follow the procedures and gently remind those who do not of the correct implementation. When the teacher makes this immediate correction, it sets a precedent for the students that this teacher really means what she says.

> *Caution: Failure to immediately correct any incorrect implementation is a sure recipe for failure, as you will see when you read how these same students behave in the classroom of Teacher B!*

Before moving on to Teacher B's classroom, you should know that Teacher A implemented many procedures on the first few days of school. Here are just a few of them:[1]

+ Taking the roll
+ Sharpening pencils
+ Getting students' attention
+ Talking in class
+ Using classroom materials and supplies
+ Distributing and collecting materials
+ Managing group work
+ Discarding trash
+ Conducting parent conferences

---

1 All of these procedures can be found in Elizabeth Breaux, *Classroom Management Simplified* (Larchmont, NY: Eye on Education, 2005).

- Calling home
- Requesting water and bathroom privileges
- Taking a test
- Providing for early finishers
- Taking responsibility for recording grades
- Attending assemblies

What Doesn't Work

 Before we move on to Teacher B's classroom, remember that both teachers have many of the same desirable teaching qualities:

- They love teaching.
- They love students.
- They are highly knowledgeable in their content area.
- They are highly qualified to teach in their content area.
- They are organized.
- They are very personable and likeable.
- They have created an inviting learning environment in their classroom.

You will notice, however, that Teacher B—even though she is teaching the same students—experiences many management problems that Teacher A does not experience. This is the result of two critical errors made by Teacher B:

1. She *assumes* (and you know what they say about that) that the students already know many of the procedures, so she skips the critical teaching and practicing steps.

2. She fails to *immediately correct the improper implementation* of certain procedures from the beginning—a big mistake!

The lunch bell rings, and the students move to Teacher B's class. They are a bit rowdy (as all students are when they come in from recess), but they eventually settle down. Teacher B doesn't want to be mean on the first day of school, so she does not address this undesirable behavior (because it was really not that flagrant anyway). Once the students finally stop talking, she begins to speak: "Good afternoon. Did you all have a good lunch?" Several students answer in unison, most complaining about the "awful food they serve us here." Once the conversation subsides, Teacher B asks if everyone has a pencil. Several do not, and they begin the hunt for a borrowed one. Three of them get out of their desks, borrow pencils from others, then head to the pencil sharpener—you know the routine. Because Teacher B is not prepared with procedures and a plan for teaching, practicing, and implementing them, the students devise several procedures for her:

- Procedure for entering the classroom: Come in talking, sit when ready, and continue talking until the teacher asks you to stop.

- Procedure for asking or answering a question: Simply blurt out the answer as loudly as possible and hope the teacher can hear you above the other students.

- Procedure for bringing or borrowing materials: If you forget your materials, it's no big deal. Simply ask around until someone lets you borrow what you need. Then get up (no need to ask permission) and borrow the item.

- Procedure for sharpening a pencil: Get up as needed. No need to ask permission. It does not matter whether the teacher is in the middle of teaching a lesson. She probably won't mind anyway.

Teacher B has unintentionally and unknowingly allowed the students to begin their own implementation of these four procedures, all in a matter of five minutes or less on the first day of school. Unfortunately, Teacher B is not familiar with the concept of how to teach, practice, and implement procedures, so this activity continues after the first day.

Teacher B ends up with a class that is totally out of control, yet she has no idea why. "Why is it that these students behave beautifully in Teacher A's class?" she keeps asking herself.

No need to expound. Suffice it to say that Teacher B has a miserable year—all because she does not realize that she has the power to set procedures in her own classroom, her way, from day one!

Summary

 If the teacher does not set procedures in the classroom, the students will do it. They will begin in the first few minutes of the first day of school. If this is allowed, it will snowball, no doubt about it. Remember that when setting procedures, you must do the following:

- Be kind
- Be assertive
- Be thankful and give lots of praise

- Spend some time teaching the procedure
- Spend some time practicing the procedure—and don't forget to encourage mistakes during this step
- Begin consistent implementation of the procedure immediately
- Correct any improper implementation when it occurs

Soon, you will find that you have many more procedures than rules guiding your classroom management. Your classroom will be a much happier and more relaxed place—an environment that is conducive to learning. What more is there?

If and Then
(For Students)

If I ask you quite politely
Then you'll oblige me, this is likely
But if I cry and whine and scream
You might turn from nice to mean

If I study really hard
Then I will get the grand reward
But if I fail to be concerned
I'll get the grade that I have earned

If I raise my hand to speak
Then you will acknowledge me
But if I speak without permission
You most likely will not listen

If I follow all the rules
Then I will have no trouble in school
But if I break them (should I dare)
You'll see me back in here next year!

Elizabeth Breaux

If and Then
(For Teachers)

If I rush in late for school
Then I'll appear to be a fool
But if I'm early and I'm ready
I'll greet the day with calm and steady

If I neglect to plan my lesson
Then I'll be improvising (guessing)
But if I plan for every minute
The students all will join me in it

If I am kind yet firm in flavor
My students will show good behavior
But if I show them disrespect
I will deserve what I will get

If I am late for a faculty meeting
Then I will get a glaring greeting
But if I arrive in timely fashion
I won't receive that staring lashing

If my principal does observe
Then I will not be balls of nerves
I'll be the one who says, "Don't ask,
Come any time, we're always on
task!"

Elizabeth Breaux

Enforcing Consequences: The "Ifs" and "Thens"

Contrary to the old saying "rules are made to be broken," the opposite is true: Rules are made to be followed! Let's face it, "ifs" and "thens" are not just for students. They are for anyone who participates in life! Because many decisions are guided by the fear of consequences, it is necessary to attach a specific consequence to the breaking of any rule. Here are some real-life examples:

- You are driving to work. The speed limit is 55 miles per hour, but everyone is going at least 65 to 70 miles per hour. You join in. Up ahead, you see a police car parked on the side of the road. What do you do?
    A. Accelerate to 85 miles per hour.
    B. Decelerate to 45 miles per hour just to be safe.
    C. Cover your eyes and pray for the best.
- You are late for work—again. Your principal has tolerated this for too long, and he finally calls you in for a formal reprimand. You are certain that he will no longer tolerate this behavior. He assures you that he will be watching from now on. What will you do?
    A. Get up 30 minutes earlier tomorrow so that you can arrive on time.
    B. Sleep late (as usual), arrive late (as usual), and mosey in through the front office, stopping in the lounge for coffee.
    C. Spend the night at school to ensure punctuality.

The fact is that in life, we make choices. If we are about to behave in a way that may send dire consequences our way, we normally choose another route, especially if we are certain that the behavior will elicit the feared consequence every time. What if, on the other hand, the behavior does not always elicit the feared consequence? Let's consider one of the previous examples:

- You are driving to work, taking the same route that you travel every day. You are driving 65 miles per hour in a 55 miles per hour zone. There is a policeman up ahead on the side of the road. He's there every single day because he directs traffic at that particular intersection when it gets hectic each morning. He is not there to issue speeding tickets (as far as you have surmised). You speed by at 65 miles per hour every single day, along with everyone else, and are never stopped. No big deal, right? Not so today! Today, as you approach, his lights go on, and he pulls you over and issues a ticket. You are furious! You can't believe it! Is he crazy?

Question: Who was wrong?
    A. You
    B. The police officer
    C. Both of you
Answer: C

Justification: You were wrong because the speed limit was 55 miles per hour. It has always been 55 miles per hour. You knew that the speed limit was 55 miles per hour, and you chose to break the law. The police officer was wrong because he should have let all drivers know from the very beginning that the 55 miles per hour speed limit sign was not part a highway beautification project! It was there for the purpose of letting drivers know the speed limit allowed by law. He was there to issue an immediate consequence in the event that the law was broken, but he did not do that.

- Your job was to follow the law!
- His job was to enforce the law!
- Neither of you did your job!

Problem: The law was not doing an adequate job of enforcing its consequence, so drivers began to take advantage.

Lesson: Students view rules and consequences in the same way adults do! If they are allowed to break the law without fear of retribution, they will continue to do so. Teachers must lay down the law and then enforce it with absolute consistency if they want their students to trust what they say.

Bottom line: A rule that is not enforced is useless. It should be enforced, or it should be done away with. Otherwise, it holds no merit.

In the previous chapter, we talked about procedures. Remember, procedures do not have consequences attached to them. In the next situation, we will look specifically at rules and their consequences.

Situation

 Tar D. High School has a problem that plagues many high schools: student tardiness. The school has a tardy policy that is dictated by the district, but many teachers complain that the tardy policy does not work. Student tardiness is rampant in many classrooms.

Standing in the hallway as the bell rings, an observer would see that the tardy policy works perfectly in some classrooms but not in others. This is evidenced by the urgency of some students to get to their classrooms on time and the nonchalant meandering of other students even after the tardy bell has rung.

Is it the policy that is inadequate, or is the implementation of the policy inadequate? Upon review, the policy seems to be quite stringent. It reads as follows:

- Tardy #1: warning, record in roll book
- Tardy #2: parent contact, record in roll book
- Tardy #3: office referral, in-school suspension
- Tardy #4: office referral, in-school suspension
- Tardy #5: office referral, in-school suspension
- Tardy #6: office referral, out-of-school suspension
- Tardy #7: office referral, out-of-school suspension
- Tardy #8: office referral, out-of-school suspension
- Tardy #9: recommended expulsion

We'll look into the classrooms of two teachers who teach in the same school and who should be implementing the same tardy policy. It works beautifully in one classroom but not in the other. Why is that?

What Works

 Ms. Timely has become such a master at implementing procedures that she has very few rules that govern her classroom. She does have a few, and she has chosen them with diligence, as they are things that *must and do have consequences* attached to them. Here are her rules:

- **Respect** others at all times.
- Be **punctual**.
- Maintain your **composure**.
- Follow the **dress code**.

Ms. Timely believes that the breaking of any of these rules should elicit an immediate (predetermined) consequence. During the first days of school, she discusses the rules with her students. She cites examples of infractions as she goes into detail about each rule. She also spells out the consequences for infractions. (Because we are at Tar D. High School, we'll look specifically at her enforcement of the tardy policy.)

"Students, I am giving to you a copy of the school district's tardy policy. You will notice that on the first infraction, you will merely receive a warning. On the second infraction, I must contact your parents so that they can be forewarned that in the event of a third infraction, you will receive an in-school suspension. You will notice that after three in-school suspensions, you will receive an out-of-school suspension, and after three out-of-school suspensions, you will be recommended for expulsion. I almost laugh every time I read this, because I cannot even imagine that any student would allow himself or herself to be recommended for expulsion because of tardiness! Not at this school, where you have five minutes to get from one class to another! I want to assure you that I do not tolerate tardiness, in myself or in my students. If you are late for class and have no excuse, you will receive a consequence. I ask that you not put me in the position of having to refer you to the office because of tardiness. Those of you who know me already know that I rarely send a student to the office, and I dread the day that I have to do just that. That being said, I would like to show you the Tardy Chart that I have created. You will notice that there are no names on the chart. There are only numbers. Everyone will be given a number. In the event that you are tardy, I will place an X next to your number so that you will always be aware of the number of tardies that you have accrued (if any). Rest assured, you will receive the consequence that has been predetermined for each level of tardiness."

Ms. Timely goes to the chart and asks the students to come closer. She wants them to get a close look at the chart. (The chart is on the wall next to the door, where all students can easily view it as they enter and exit each day.) "You will notice that the chart is numbered from 1 to 125. I teach 125 students this year, and each of you will have your own number. I will give you a number, but I will share it with no one else. It is your choice as to whether you share your number with others." (See the sample Tardy Chart on page 41.)

Like all students, some tested Ms. Timely during the first few days of school to determine whether she was for real! They determined that she *was* for real. On the second day of school, two students were late for class. When they arrived the following day, an X had been placed next to each of their names. One of the two was tardy the following day as well, and a second X was placed next to his name. Ms. Timely called his mother during her planning period that day. She told his mother that a third infraction would force her to send him to the office, where he would receive an in-school suspension. His mother assured Ms. Timely that she would "take care of it" when he got home. This follow-through on the part of Ms. Timely also set a precedent for others when they heard that Ms. Timely really does call parents!

There was an occasional tardy from time to time throughout the year, and Ms. Timely simply handled it exactly as she said she would. Several students were sent to the office and received in-school suspensions, but none was ever sent home for tardiness. All of the students learned their lesson long before that. They also learned that Ms. Timely meant what she said and that she was fair. The chart served two very important purposes:

1. It raised the awareness of the students. Those who accrued two tardies knew that a third infraction would earn them a trip to the office, so they just didn't do it.

2. It served as proof! You see, in the past, a student who had been sent to the office would normally be angry with the teacher, saying things such as, "Why did you send me to the office? I wasn't tardy three times!" However, thanks to the chart, the students are always aware of the number of infractions.

In Ms. Timely's classroom, the door closed with the ringing of the tardy bell, and she began class immediately. The tardy policy worked for her because she worked with the tardy policy, plain and simple!

What Doesn't Work

 Ms. D'Lay wants her students to be on time for class, but her lack of punctuality in the past has served as a model of exactly the opposite behavior. In fact, her students are often seen waiting in the hallway for her to arrive and unlock the door! Realizing that she needs to change her behavior, Ms. D'Lay decides that she will turn over a new leaf this year. She will be punctual, and so will her students.

Like Ms. Timely, Ms. D'Lay begins by giving each student a copy of the tardy policy. She tells them to read it and take it home for their parents to review. And that is the end of that—a big mistake.

On the second day of school, several students are late for class. Ms. D'Lay gives them a verbal warning, but she does not make a note of the infractions. The following day, several students are again tardy. Again, Ms. D'Lay warns them, but again, no notation is made. Ms. D'Lay is noticeably upset the following day when students arrive later and later. She begins to ask the question, "Why are you late for class?" (Huge mistake. If you ask a question, you will get an answer. The truth is that Ms. D'Lay probably doesn't care why they are late anyway. So why ask?) Now, because she has asked a question, several conversations begin, a couple of which turn into power struggles.

This goes on for a couple of weeks until Ms. D'Lay can stand it no more. "No more warnings! This has gotten to be ridiculous. You all have five minutes to get from one class to another, so why are so many of you coming in late?" (Another "why" question, and more answers.) "I am going to start writing up people today. I'm warning you that several of you will be called to the office, so don't be surprised when it happens. And you know who you are."

Ms. D'Lay completes several office referral forms during her planning period that day. The problem is that she has no documentation. She is certain that these students were tardy at least three or more times, but she has no paper trail. She has also neglected to make any home contacts, as is indicated in step two of the tardy policy. When the principal receives the referrals, she cannot enforce the consequence for step three (in-school suspension) because step two was never enforced. Therefore, she must return the referrals to Ms. D'Lay and ask for documentation of the dates of infractions and the dates of parental contacts, which Ms. D'Lay cannot give her. Ms. D'Lay is unhappy because, she believes, the tardy policy doesn't work.

Summary

 Once again, we see that rules are made to be followed! Ms. Timely and Ms. D'Lay both teach at Tar D. High School, both teach many of the same students, and both must follow the same tardy policy. Remember, too, that the students have five minutes between classes…all classes. Both teachers experience quite different results, however. Let's examine why:

- ♦ Ms. Timely gave each student a copy of the tardy policy and discussed it on the first day of school. She also created a Tardy Chart (see page 41) for the students and displayed and discussed it with them. She implemented the consequences exactly as the policy dictated, and she did so the very first time that students were tardy. She continued to implement the consequences until all students realized there was no way around it—Ms. Timely was for real!

- ♦ Ms. D'Lay gave each student a copy of the tardy policy on the first day of school, but she spent no time discussing it. As students began to arrive late, she simply gave verbal warnings. She did not record tardiness, nor did she follow the process for step two: calling parents. The students soon realized that Ms. D'Lay would not follow the policy, so they continued to be late for class. Once things had gotten totally out of control, Ms. D'Lay decided to refer several students to the office. Without documentation, however, step three could not be enforced. Ms. D'Lay's immediate reaction was that the policy just didn't work.

Ms. Timely implemented the policy exactly as dictated by the district, beginning on the first day of school, and she remained consistent in her implementation. Ms. D'Lay, too, remained consistent in her implementation, though hers was incorrect and ineffective.

Ms. Timely's students were on time for class, whereas Ms. D'Lay's students were not. Same school, same policy, but different implementations and very different results.

Bottom line: Do not "D'Lay!" Begin the "Timely" implementation of policy immediately!

Figure 5.1. Tardy Chart

Student	1 Warning	2 Call parent	3 Office referral, in-school suspension	4 Office referral, in-school suspension	5 Office referral, in-school suspension	6 Office referral, out-of-school suspension	7 Office referral, out-of-school suspension	8 Office referral, out-of-school suspension	9 Office referral, recommended expulsion
1	X								
2									
3									
4									
5									
6	X	X							
7	X	X	X						
8									
9									
10									
11									
12									
13	X	X	X						
14									
15									
16									
17									
18									
19	X								
20									

A Teacher's Oath

I, the teacher, promise to take your child and hold him securely under my wing. I will love, nurture, care for, protect, and teach him to the best of my ability. I will share his sorrows and pains, his joys and his successes. I will be proud of him and of the job that I will do to assist him on his journey. I will choose to like him even when he is difficult. I will choose to differentiate between "bad actions" and "bad people." I will never become a victim of him, nor will I ever allow him to be victimized by me. I will be firm, kind, fair, and consistent. I will treat him as my own, giving him no less than the best that I have to give. I will become allies with those who love him the most, his parents, and bond with them in their endeavor to mold him into all that he is capable of becoming. At the end of the year, I will send him on his way without regret, for I will know that I have done my small part in giving him the tools that he needs to become a productive, contributing member of society. I will cry as he leaves me, both tears of sadness (for I will know that my job has been completed) and tears of joy (for I will know that I completed it well).

Elizabeth Breaux

Making Home Contacts: Getting Parents on Your Side

Parents can be a teacher's greatest ally or most feared foe. When parents are on our side, great feats can be accomplished. When we perceive them as adversaries, however, we feel limited in our ability to help students fulfill their potential.

It is a rare parent who would not be a strong ally of a teacher who subscribes to the philosophy in "A Teacher's Oath." Parents, however, must first be given the opportunity. Sadly, many parents are not, especially in high-risk and low-performing schools, in which parent involvement tends to be low. Often, the reason is that teachers don't take the first strides to involve parents because they automatically assume the parents don't care. The truth is, if teachers don't take the first strides, many parents will not either.

I have often heard teachers complain about the lack of parental involvement. I've heard them say such things as

- ◆ "The parents don't care."
- ◆ "I can't contact anyone. They don't answer their phones when they know it is the school calling."
- ◆ "You can't even get them to sign a paper."
- ◆ "Have you ever met his mother? How can you expect any more of him?"
- ◆ "Open House was a joke. The parents who needed to come didn't."

In many cases, if teachers want parents to become involved, they need to take the first steps. Stop waiting for the parents to come to you. Many will not. Many are actually afraid of becoming involved or don't know how to become involved. Many parents will tell you that they only hear from the school when there is a problem. If that is the case, no wonder they are afraid to answer the phone!

If we teachers call home only to discuss negative behavior, then we are setting ourselves up for a bad situation, and we often are afraid to make that call. It's not comfortable or easy, and often we are happy when no one answers! We do have the power to change this. We can initiate contact with parents at any time—the sooner the better—and to praise positive behavior. If we do that, we are ensuring two things:

1. It will be a positive, pleasant call, and the parents will feel that they know us and that we are on their side.

2. If we ever need to call because of negative behavior, they will be on our side!

But how do you call parents to praise positive behaviors if a child doesn't do anything positive? Find something positive! And don't wait until the negatives start to seem insurmountable. Start during the first week or two of school, when students usually give us lots of opportunities to make positive home contacts.

Situation

Parental involvement has traditionally been low at this elementary school. It is one of the lower performing schools in the district, and low parental involvement has been cited as one of the underlying causes. Most teachers assume little involvement on the part of the parents, so they are not surprised from year to year when this continues to be the norm. It's what they already expect.

In an attempt to entice more parents to become involved in their children's education, the district has prescribed an action plan that is to be implemented during this new school year. The plan is presented to the teachers during a staff development session at the beginning of the school year. Many teachers seem a little apprehensive, but most agree to give it their best shot. Unfortunately, however, some do not.

What Works

Mrs. Believe has taught at this low-performing elementary school for 21 years, and she understands the issue of parental involvement as well as anyone. Year after year, she has dealt with (what she believed was) student and parent apathy. She has just been motivated, however, to try to reach out to and involve parents once again. Even though she feels that she has tried everything possible, the staff development meeting that she has just attended has given her a new outlook and inner motivation to try something new.

Mrs. Believe makes a vow to herself that she will try these new strategies and continue to implement them throughout the school year. She feels that, in the past, she gave up long before new strategies had a chance to prove their value. She opens up the strategies handbook that she just has received in the staff development meeting, and she begins to read some of the "Tips for Getting Parents Involved":

- ◆ For every student you teach, commit to making a positive parent contact during the first few weeks of the new school year.
- ◆ Divide the number of students you teach by the number of days that you can commit to making calls home. For example, if you teach 50 students, give yourself about two weeks (10 school days). You will have to call five parents per day to finish within the two-week time frame. If you teach 25 students (as you might if you are a self-contained elementary teacher), you may want to contact five parents a day and finish in one work week.

- On the first day of school, verify the students' contact information. Sometimes telephone numbers, e-mail addresses, and mailing addresses have changed. Students are very willing to give you the correct information during those first days. (If you wait to ask for the contact information once a problem arises, you may be given the number for Joe's Pool Hall.)

- Commit to using part of your before-school time, your planning time, your lunch time, or your after-school time on the days that you will be calling home. However, evenings should be left open for calling only parents whom you were unable to contact during the school day.

- Make a list of positive comments that could apply to any student. Before making the call, pick one or two (or more) that apply to the given student. Your list could look something like this:
  - Your child is very polite.
  - Your child is very cooperative.
  - Your child obeys school rules.
  - Your child follows procedures willingly.
  - Your child is very helpful to me and to other students.
  - Your child is usually on task.
  - Your child is a hard worker.
  - Your child has a lot of potential.
  - Your child is attentive.
  - Your child does his or her homework.
  - Your child is organized.
  - Your child is creative.
  - Your child enjoys reading.
  - Your child apologizes when he or she makes a mistake.
  - Your child is a good leader.
  - Your child works well in groups.
  - Your child makes friends easily.
  - Your child respects authority.

- Plan your dialogue. You don't need to be on the phone for 30 minutes with each parent. I have found that beginning the conversation in this way works beautifully:

  "Good morning Mrs. Johnson, this is Mrs. Believe, Jason's history teacher. I apologize if I am disturbing you. I know that you must be quite busy, so I won't keep you long."

By telling the parent that you won't keep him or her long because you know they are busy, you are indicating immediately that this will be a quick, unobtrusive call. You can then proceed to complete the conversation by saying something like this:

"I just wanted you to know that I am so happy to have Jason in my class this year. What a hard worker he is! He has done everything I've asked of him so far. He is really attentive, too, and always on task. I'm just calling to let you know that you are more than welcome to call me at any time or to come in for a conference. My planning period is from 9:30 to 10:30, and I'm also available before or after school any day. We're planning a field trip at the end of the month and could use some help. If Jason's organizational skills are any indication of yours, we could definitely use your help!"

Note: Mrs. Johnson surely will have some input during this conversation (once she recovers from the fainting spell and picks herself up off the floor), so the conversation could take 5 to 10 minutes, but it is worth every minute. Let this be a bonding time. If you ever have to call back with bad news, you won't be so hesitant to call, and Mrs. Johnson will be on your side and willing to help! Remember the old phrase "saved by the bell"? If Mrs. Johnson just won't let you off the phone, you can always use the excuse that the bell is about to ring!

- Once all of your initial calls are made, plan for subsequent positive calls. You could commit to calling one parent per day with good news for the remainder of the year. Even if you teach a large number of students, each parent will still get more positive calls than they've received throughout the duration of their child's years in school.

- Create a list of ways that you could elicit parents' help, and use this during your subsequent phone calls. Once parents get to know you, they will be much more likely to volunteer. If you give them the impression that you welcome and need their help, they will feel needed and will be more likely to offer their services.

Mrs. Believe reads through these tips and begins planning her implementation. She begins the implementation on the first day of school and stays true to her vow not to waiver during the year. She soon realizes that by assuming the best in her students from the very beginning and by immediately sharing her observations with their parents, she makes considerably fewer negative home contacts. She just doesn't have to.

During the next year, she decides that in addition to the calls, she will start mailing "good news" letters home on a weekly basis. She finds that mailing one letter per week is easily accomplished. (The gesture means much more if it is mailed than if it is given to the student to deliver. Plus, you have the assurance of knowing that the letter is making it all the way home and into the hands of the parents.)

Mrs. Believe even starts to notice that students and parents wait for the contacts. Many actually schedule parent–teacher conferences, which Mrs. Believe soon turns in to parent–teacher–student conferences. At the end of the year, Mrs. Believe ponders years passed and how she normally felt at the end of those years. She realizes that the extra time that she has committed to eliciting more parental involvement has paid huge dividends, and they have all—students, parents, and teachers—been benefactors. She also realizes that it is within her power to entice parents to become more involved in the educational lives of their children. She can't wait until next year—and all because Mrs. Believe made a commitment and decided to believe.

What Doesn't Work

 Mr. Skeptic works in the same school as Mrs. Believe and has done so for 18 years. He has learned to accept the lack of parental involvement as a fact of life, one that he has no control over or power to change. He has just attended the same staff development meeting as Mrs. Believe, but he leaves with a totally different outlook. He leans over to his fellow teacher, Mrs. Skeptic, and asks, "What next? We already teach these kids. Now they want us to parent them, too. Will we have to clothe and shelter them next year? If the parents don't care, why should we? I must have missed the part about the extra pay for the extra work that they're asking us to do."

Mr. Skeptic proceeds to begin his school year as he has in past years. He does not make one positive parent contact. He does not call home until a problem has gotten totally out of hand, and when he does, his attitude and tone of voice put parents on the defensive. Instead of eliciting further parental involvement, his actions (or lack thereof) ensure that parental involvement remains at its current low level.

Mr. Skeptic, once again, uses his tried-and-true excuse for why the students in his classes fail academically: "Parents simply don't care."

Summary

 Parents truly can be a teacher's greatest ally or most feared foe. When parents are on our side, great feats can be accomplished. When we perceive them as adversaries, we allow ourselves to be limited in our ability to help students achieve their potential. If we truly want to stimulate parental involvement in our schools and in our classrooms, we must make these commitments:

- We must choose to believe that all parents truly care about their child's education, regardless of whether we feel that their actions portray this.

- We must choose to believe that we have the power to bring even the most reluctant of parents to the table.

- We must realize that many parents' experiences with the school have been only negative, and this is what they have come to expect. They simply have never had anyone call with anything good to say about their children.

- We must commit to being the one who initiates the positive interaction, knowing that it is not likely to occur otherwise.

- We must go through the steps (as Mrs. Believe did) with persistence, resolve, determination, and consistency.

By choosing to be relentless in our endeavor, teachers, parents, and students all reap the benefits. We cannot force parents to become more involved in the education of their children, but we can open the door and welcome them in. We must believe that we have the power to increase parental involvement and make it a positive experience. We must not allow ourselves to become skeptics, for when we do, we all lose.

> *If I want you to act kindly*
> *I must do the same*
> *But if I model cruelty*
> *I will expect disdain.*
>
> *If I'd like for you to yell at me*
> *I assure you that you'll know*
> *For I will model screaming*
> *And then watch your temper blow.*
>
> *I'll scream at you and you'll scream back*
> *A natural reaction*
> *I'll trade my words for each of yours*
> *A deplorable transaction.*
>
> *So I must choose to model*
> *What I expect from you*
> *Then in return I'm sure to earn*
> *Respect for me, from you.*
>
> Elizabeth Breaux

Avoiding Power Struggles: Everybody Wins

I used to make a promise to my students every year that I would never raise my voice in anger at them. I knew that if I made the promise, they would hold me to it! I let them know that I also expected the same in return. I realized that I needed to set myself up for success and that making such a promise would be a good start toward achieving my goal: to never engage in a power struggle with a student.

Power struggles occur when two people feel that an issue is open for negotiation. A person who does not have the skills to negotiate in an adult fashion may resort to a heightened tone of voice, name calling, and accusations, all of which actually prevent the issue from ever being resolved. Because neither person has the skills necessary to resolve the issue, the two begin vying for power (hence the screaming, name calling, and accusing). The truth is that in student–teacher relationships, some things are simply nonnegotiable.

Many students do not know how to handle conflicting viewpoints. Too often, the incorrect way has been modeled for them at home and, unfortunately, at school. They have seen far too many adults handle conflict in inappropriate ways, and that's all they know. Teachers must *never* allow power struggles to occur between themselves and their students—absolutely and unconditionally. It's really quite simple. It takes two to have a power struggle: If a student tries to engage you, simply do not take part.

Here are some questions that I often wish I could ask teachers who are screamers:

- Do you mind if students scream at you?
- Do you think that it is appropriate for students to scream at one another?
- Do you think that it is appropriate for your principal to scream at you during a faculty meeting (or at any time)?
- Do you think that it is appropriate for one of your fellow teachers to scream at you, even if you have done something really terrible?

I assume that most teachers would answer no to all of the above. For those teachers, then, I would have one last question: Why, then, is it ever appropriate for a teacher to scream at a student?

Many power struggles between teachers and students occur the moment the teacher gives the child the impression that an issue is negotiable. Here is an example: A teacher goes over the rules, and all students are clear on the "ifs" and "thens." A child breaks a rule and the teacher issues a consequence. End of story, right? Not so if the teacher allows negotiation. Here's an example of what can happen if a teacher allows negotiation in a situation that is supposed to be nonnegotiable:

- The teacher reprimands the student and issues a consequence.
- The student asks, "Why?"
- The teacher responds, answering the question in a heightened and aggravated tone of voice.
- The student tries to bargain with the teacher and answers back.
- The teacher responds again in a more heightened tone of voice.
- The student again does not elicit the response that he or she wants and begins to argue with the teacher in the heightened tone of voice that the teacher has been modeling.

- This power struggle goes on and on as long as the teacher continues to engage!

Let's consider a situation in which the teacher chooses not to engage at all. It truly is the teacher's choice. It takes two to have an argument. (It's not much fun to argue with yourself, even though you do have a much greater chance of winning!)

- Jody is late for class…again.
- The teacher records the offense.
- Jody sees this and says, "I'm not tardy! I was helping Mrs. Jones clean up after the lab experiment!"
- The teacher has a choice about whether to engage or not to engage. She chooses not to engage.
- "Oh, no problem, Jody. I'll just mark the tardy in pencil until I get a note from Mrs. Jones and then I'll erase it." The teacher immediately moves on to teaching.

By answering Jody in this way, the teacher avoided a power struggle. She defused the situation. Jody did not have a rebuttal. In fact, the teacher assumed that Jody was telling her the truth and gave her a chance to bring a note and have the tardy erased. (The teacher knows Jody quite well and knows that she was in the hallway with her boyfriend. Jody won't bring a note tomorrow, and the teacher certainly will not ask for one. The teacher is covered because she told Jody that she would erase it once the excuse was given to her.)

It's really quite simple—in theory, anyway. If an issue is nonnegotiable, don't negotiate! If a situation is negotiable, do it in private. Most students will put on an Academy Award –winning performance if given an audience!

NOTE: It is possible to engage in a power struggle in which no screaming takes place. This is still lethal because the problem cannot be resolved once the issue becomes power instead of the resolution of the problem. If this happens, the issue is often lost amid the struggle for power. In my experience, most teachers who engage in power struggles allow the struggle to continue until it reaches a point at which screaming takes place.

Situation

I was called in to observe a new teacher, Mrs. Robinson, whom I was told was struggling. This new teacher had gone to her principal to ask for help. The principal called me to see whether I could offer some assistance. When I told her that I would be happy to do that, she gave Mrs. Robinson my contact information, and she got in touch with me herself. We decided on a day when I would come in strictly to conduct a very informal observation. I wanted to see the class in action before helping the teacher find a remedy.

Mrs. Robinson had accepted this teaching position and entered a classroom in which there had been several previous teachers. It was the middle of the year, so the students had been given little or no consistent structure that year. I was extremely impressed with the candor of this new teacher. She had realized that she was struggling and asked for help—any help!

In this chapter, first we will look at what doesn't work (what I observed during the first observation) and then we will look at what works (what I observed during the second observation).

> *Note: After my first observation, the principal was kind enough to hire a substitute to take Mrs. Robinson's class one day. During that time, she and I met and designed a plan, which she began implementing immediately after the meeting. The results were evident during my second observation.*

What Doesn't Work

I arrived to observe this fifth-grade class at the scheduled time. Mrs. Robinson was aware and happy that I was coming. We had previously agreed that I would come in for an informal observation, and we would meet at a later time to discuss the observation and devise a plan of action. I walked to the back of the room, where I sat, observed, and took notes for about an hour. After just a few minutes in the room, I was certain of several things:

- ◆ This was *not* a bad class.
- ◆ Mrs. Robinson had the potential to be an excellent teacher.
- ◆ Mrs. Robinson loved her students.
- ◆ Mrs. Robinson was knowledgeable in the subject matter.

- Mrs. Robinson wanted order in the classroom so that she could teach; she just wasn't certain how to create it.
- Mrs. Robinson did not have a solid management plan in place—or if she did, it was not being implemented consistently.

Mrs. Robinson had a well-planned lesson in place, which she followed as best she could. The many disruptions, however, ruined any chance for effective implementation of the lesson. Mrs. Robinson had to "put out fires" throughout the lesson. I had trouble following along because of the interruptions, so I was certain that little learning was occurring. Here are some of the observations that I made:

- Mrs. Robinson had trouble getting the students settled so that class could begin. She had to ask several times for the talking to stop. The students responded to her (initially) and were not disrespectful, but the behavior soon reoccurred, prompting her to ask over and over again for the talking to stop.
- While she was teaching, the students got out of their chairs for various reasons: to borrow materials from others, to sharpen their pencils, or to throw away trash. Each time, she would direct them to return to their desks. After a while, she began asking, "Why are you out of your desk? You know you are not supposed to do that." The students, of course, would answer the question, she would respond, and on and on…
- The students began talking at will while she was teaching. She would stop teaching and ask them to stop talking. This happened over and over. Then, she asked one student (who was obviously unhappy with the young lady seated behind him) to turn around. "Make her stop!" screamed the young man. "Tell her to stop touching me!" Mrs. Robinson stopped the class and attempted to uncover the great mystery of what was going on between these two fifth-graders. This took about five precious class minutes. I don't think the mystery was ever solved.
- One young man never did take out his class materials. Mrs. Robinson walked over to him on a couple of occasions and told him to get to work; he never did, and she never came back. His desk remained bare during the entire time that I was there. Several other students were off task several times during that period. One cleaned out her desk. (It actually looked really nice by the time I left!)

Mrs. Robinson was teaching the entire time, but the lesson was so fragmented by all of the disruptions that it was ineffective. Mrs. Robinson, amazingly, managed to maintain her composure the entire time. She did not manage, however, to avoid power struggles. When she asked the students to stop talking, the talking continued. When she asked them to stay at their desks, they continued walking around the room. When she asked them to get to work, some of them refused.

The entire class period was a power struggle between the teacher and the students over who would get their way, and the students were winning. (That's ironic because in order to win, they must forfeit their education. Let's just say they were winning the battle but losing the war.)

When I am observing a teacher who is struggling, I take notes in the form of questions that I can ask the teacher during our postobservation meeting. Here are some of the questions that I wrote down:

◆ How would you like the students to enter the room each morning?

◆ What is your procedure for getting the students' attention?

◆ Is it alright with you if students get out of their seats to sharpen pencils, borrow materials, or throw away trash without asking permission?

◆ Is it alright with you if students talk while you are teaching?

◆ Do you want your students to be on task?

Plan of Action

Mrs. Robinson and I met the following day. Invariably, when I ask a new teacher the questions that I wrote down during my observation, he or she always gives the obvious answers. Mrs. Robinson told me that she would like the students to enter the room quietly each morning, go directly to their desks, and begin the bell work. She said that she did not want the students to leave their desks at any time without permission and that there should be no talking while the teacher is teaching. She expected all the students to be on task and to follow her instructions.

I took all of her information, and together we devised a plan. Mrs. Robinson made a list of 10 problem areas that she wanted to address. She decided that if she created and *effectively implemented* a procedure for these 10 areas, she could finally teach her class and avoid the power struggles that were occurring daily.

1. Enter class without talking and go directly to your desk.
2. Begin bell work immediately.
3. Raise your hand to ask a question.
4. Ask permission to leave your desk.

5. Give the "pencil signal" when sharpening is needed. The teacher will give you one of her pencils, take your pencil, sharpen your pencil for you, and then trade back.

6. Place trash on the corner of your desk. The teacher will retrieve it while she is walking around the room. Any leftovers should be discarded when you exit the room.

7. Transitions will be timed.

8. Homework will be turned in daily.

9. Stay on task.

10. Clean your space before leaving the room.

Because this particular class had been allowed to implement procedures in their own way for such a long time, Mrs. Robinson and I felt that giving the students some incentive to begin the proper implementation might hasten the process. Mrs. Robinson told me that she would create a Weekly Points Chart (including only these 10 items) for daily procedures. The checklist would be given to each student on the first day of each week (see the sample on page 60). She would explain to the students that beginning that day, they would receive 10 points per day (for a total of 50 points per week), but any infraction would cost them one point. Students with at least 45 points at the end of each week would be allowed to use their points to purchase "School Bucks," which could be used to buy items from the school's supply store. She told me that she would take one class period to explain everything to them and then begin immediate implementation.

Before I left, I told her that the plan was excellent but that its effectiveness would be in her hands. She would have to be *consistent* in her implementation if she wanted it to work. She would have to convince the students that these are nonnegotiable items. She would have to commit to *no more negotiation*, which would result in *no more power struggles*. (I also told her that I would give her a couple of weeks before returning.)

What Works

 It was a miracle! (Or was it simply the consistent implementation of a concrete plan?) I arrived about two weeks after my first visit. When I walked into the room, the students looked happy. (I realized that I had not seen that in many of their faces on the first visit.) Again, I walked to the back of the room and sat down to observe. This is what I saw:

♦ I saw that each child had a Weekly Points Chart on his or her desk, off to the side so as not to interfere with class work.

- All students were on task, even those who had not been on task during my first visit.
- Students were raising their hands to ask questions. At one point, a student inadvertently called out to Mrs. Robinson. She continued teaching, walked over to him, subtracted a point from his chart, and then whispered something to him. (I had advised her that if and when a student committed an infraction, she should immediately, but without fanfare, issue the penalty or else the students would begin to minimize the importance of the chart.)
- Students did not leave their desks without permission. (A couple of times, I saw students begin to leave their desks, catch themselves, and hurry back to their seats.)
- The teacher was teaching the lesson without interruption.

After about 30 minutes, I stood up to leave. As I reached the door, I knew that I just could not leave the room without complimenting the students. I asked Mrs. Robinson whether she would mind if I spoke to them for a few minutes. She was more than happy for me to do so.

"Wow!" I said to them. "Do you all remember me?" (They all nodded that they did.) "I was in here a couple of weeks ago, and I cannot believe that this is the same class." (All were by smiling now.) "I just can't seem to figure out what it is." (Of course, I was lying! I knew precisely what it was.) "Would someone like to tell me what has changed since I was last here?" Almost all of the students' hands were waiving for me to call on them. I called on one young man, and he proceeded to explain the use of the Weekly Points Chart to me. He actually explained it quite well. "We have a sheet," he said, "And if we do everything right that is on here, we get 10 points a day. And even if we lose a few, we still get a prize." "And what is the prize?" I asked. "We get to buy bucks to use at the school store!"

My wheels were spinning, and I wanted to make a point, so I used this opportunity. "From what I just observed, I'll bet that you would behave this well even if you weren't getting the points," I said to them. (Of course, all heads were nodding in agreement.) "You see," I said, "I have found that when I do the right thing, I just feel better and I smile more. I'll bet that if I followed you into your next class, you would be behaving just as well as you are in here." (All heads were still nodding in agreement.)

The truth is, these students would behave this well for anyone who is kind to them, presents a fair plan, and implements it consistently, day in and day out. The real prize should go to Mrs. Robinson.

Summary

This is the kind of teacher that our students and our schools need more of today. She realized that her classes were beginning to control her, that she was engaging more and more in day-to-day power struggles with her students. She didn't know how to reverse or fix the problem, so she asked for help. She did not blame the students, the administration, past teachers, or parents because she knew that it was within her power to manage her own classroom. She just needed the same assistance that all of us needed when we first started out. Not only did she ask for help, but also she willingly and thankfully trusted the advice of someone who had once been in her shoes.

Remember that in any situation that is nonnegotiable, don't negotiate. It's that simple. If there is a consequence for an infraction, implement it as stated. Do not bargain, or students will begin to believe that negotiation or bargaining is an option. Be consistent. It is within your power to choose whether to continue or not to continue proper implementation on a consistent basis.

Mrs. Robinson was simply being consistent. It was not the dangling of the prize that kept students accountable, but Mrs. Robinson's consistency in implementing the procedures. By using the points system and implementing it consistently, Mrs. Robinson stopped negotiating matters that never should have been negotiated in the first place. Power struggles ceased to exist.

Figure 7.1. Weekly Points Chart

Name _____	Week _____

Students will lose one point for every infraction that is committed.

Earn 45–50 points by the end of the week and use them to buy School Bucks!

1. Enter class without talking and go directly to your desk.
2. Begin bell work immediately.
3. Raise your hand to ask a question.
4. Ask permission to leave your desk.
5. Give the "pencil signal" when sharpening is needed.
6. Place trash on the corner of your desk or throw it away when exiting the room.
7. Transitions will be timed.
8. Homework will be turned in daily.
9. Stay on task.
10. Clean your space before leaving room.

Monday	Tuesday	Wednesday	Thursday	Friday	Total
~~10~~ ~~9~~ 8	~~10~~ 9	10	10	10	50 possible 47 earned

Note: This student apparently tested the teacher on Monday and Tuesday, only to realize that the teacher was going to be consistent with the implementation.

Our classroom doesn't have a front
A middle, back, or side
My teacher moves around so much
Each day's a brand new ride

We're never sure what to expect
She seems to love surprise
She's here and there and back and forth
She's psychic, clairvoyant, (or wise)

She always knows what's going on
And asks us lots of questions
She loves to read our papers
And give us cool suggestions.

She says "good job" or "get to work"
Her compliments are likely
But if she sees we're not on task
She nudges us politely.

You'd think she'd be exhausted
But she really doesn't show it
Oops! She's fallen, once again
(And she doesn't even know it!)

Elizabeth Breaux

The Mobile Teacher: Being Everywhere

Teachers must be everywhere! The most highly effective teachers in the profession probably walk miles per day without even leaving the confines of their classrooms. They know they must be close by and available to teach, help, and encourage their students. If students didn't need them, there would be no need to show up each day!

Not only do the students need teachers, but also their futures depend on them. My rule of thumb has always been that *students should leave my room each day having learned something that they did not know when they entered.* If that is not the case, then I have not done my job, plain and simple.

Teachers cannot reach and teach students if they disengage from them. Unfortunately, many teachers disengage in a variety of ways:

♦ They give busywork that keeps students occupied while they are doing something else. (Even if the "something else" is school related, there is still no teaching going on.)

♦ They give an assignment or project that requires little or no input from the teacher. (Again, no teaching is going on.)

♦ They give free time in which students are to keep themselves occupied in a variety of ways that require no effort on the part of the teacher. (Still, no teaching is going on.)

It is very hard to effectively teach a class while sitting behind a desk. One obvious reason is that the teacher's desk becomes a physical barrier between the teacher and the students. Teachers who position themselves at the teacher's desk during a large percentage of the time in class are far removed from students who do not sit near the teacher's desk. Students know that. That's why many choose to sit in the back of the classroom if possible. But if you remove the front, back, and middle of the room by becoming a highly mobile teacher, there is no way for students to get away from you!

If someone were to walk into your classroom today and ask your students where you stand to teach, could the students give a definite answer? If they could, then you are not moving around enough. If they could not, then you are a highly mobile teacher. I used to have a roll cart (the kind that holds multimedia equipment) that I could roll around with me. Sometimes I was in front, sometimes in the back, but most of the time I was right in the middle of the room, moving from one student to the next as needed. Students never knew where I was going to be. They couldn't get away from me if they tried!

The degree to which you value yourself and the importance you place on your role can be key. We all know teachers who stay glued to their seats for the majority of the year. These teachers cannot possibly value their own worth in the classroom or have any idea just how badly they are needed. "But some teachers may have a physical disability that keeps them from being highly mobile," you may be thinking. Let me give you an example that might change your mind.

Donna Rougeau, one of our profession's greatest assets, is a seventh-grade math teacher. Donna is a veteran teacher who is nearing retirement. She is highly respected by her peers, her superiors, and her students. Donna is always moving around the classroom.

Several years ago, Donna fell while walking her dog and broke her leg. The break was a severe one. She was hospitalized for a while. When she returned, she did so in a wheelchair. I can remember walking into her classroom and seeing her maneuvering in and out of the aisles in that wheelchair. It was obviously not an easy task, but Donna knew she couldn't teach effectively if she physically disengaged from her students. I vividly remember seeing her students pushing that wheelchair down the long hallway so that Donna could get to her team meeting or lunch duty. Donna never once used her injury as an excuse; instead, whether she knew it or not, she was an example to everyone around her.

Thinking about this brings back memories of others like Donna who have returned to work after surgery or an injury. The efforts they made to refrain from creating physical barriers between themselves and their students are hard to forget.

The reason you want to be highly mobile is not that you can catch students doing bad things but that you can catch them doing all of the good things they will inevitably do if they know that you are watching. If you're moving around the room, you'll know who's on task and who needs your assistance. You'll know whether your directions were clear. You'll have the opportunity to compliment the great things that you see. You'll be able to gently nudge those who need nudging. You *will not* be the teacher whose students fail because they don't do their work. You *will not* be the teacher who sits down at night to grade papers, only to realize that several are blank!

Situation

All of the seventh-grade language arts teachers in this school follow the same curriculum. At the end of each unit, all students are given the same test. For the last two years, the students in Mrs. Mover's class have turned in the highest scores in the school. For the last two years, the students in Mrs. Stationary's class have turned in the lowest scores in the school. After an in-depth review, the following facts were uncovered:

- Mrs. Mover's students have an overall 90% class average.
- Mrs. Stationary's students have an overall 71% class average.
- Mrs. Mover has referred a total of five students to the office in two years.
- Mrs. Stationary has referred a total of 122 students to the office in two years.
- According to administrative observations, Mrs. Mover is always actively involved in the lessons that she teaches.
- According to administrative observations, Mrs. Stationary is rarely seen not sitting at her desk. (She jumps up and starts to teach when an administrator walks into the room.)

Before we look into the classrooms of these two teachers, it is important to know that these are regular education classes. Again, both are seventh-grade language arts classes. Same school, same level of students, same curriculum, and same test—but very different results!

What Works

 Mrs. Mover studies the curriculum for an upcoming unit on "Reading and Responding to Literature." It is a six-week unit that concludes with a test requiring students to read passages from unfamiliar stories and then respond to critical-thinking questions. In other words, they must be able to read the material and comprehend, analyze, and apply what they have read. Her students' past test scores indicate that they are below average in their ability to read and respond to literature. Mrs. Mover knows that her students will require intense instruction using a variety of teaching methods.

She begins by choosing several short stories that are of high interest to this grade level. Her first lesson begins with a modeling exercise. Mrs. Mover knows that she must first acquire the students' interest before she can attempt to teach them. She begins by telling them a story about Gis, her 14-year-old Chihuahua, whom she had recently lost to illness. She tells them stories of Gis's life, and she walks around the room showing pictures of Gis and her other animals to the students. She tells them about the day she learned that Gis had cancer and how she had promised him that she would not allow him to suffer. She cries as she details the day she took Gis to the veterinarian to fulfill the promise that she had made to him. She cries when she tells them of her wrenching heartache and her overwhelming peace when it was all over.

She tells the students that the story they are about to read is very similar—that she and Rachel, the main character, have a lot in common. She asks whether any of the students have ever had a similar experience, and three students raise their hands to share their stories. Following this discussion, Mrs. Mover asks the students to open their books to page 47. She asks them to follow along as she reads the first paragraph. With her book in hand, Mrs. Mover begins to read as she maneuvers in and out of the aisles:

It was a day Rachel would always remember but would spend the rest of her life trying to forget. The memory of him lying there in his stillness would remain embedded in her vision forever. He had been hers since he was only four weeks old, and she had cared for him as though he had been her very own child. She could remember that day, four years prior, when she had found him alone in the rain, standing in the middle of a muddy road. She had wrapped him in her jacket and swaddled him close to her body to keep him warm. At first, her mother had not been as happy about the new pup as Rachel had been, but that did not last long. Soon, her mother loved him as much as did Rachel.

When Mrs. Mover finishes reading the first paragraph, she stops and directs the students' attention to the large whiteboard, where she has written the following question:

As the story begins, what do you think has just happened? Give evidence from the story to support your answer.

Mrs. Mover reads the question aloud as she moves closer to John's desk. "John, how many parts are there to question 1?" "Two parts," replies John. "If there are two parts, as John says, what is the first part, Sharel?" (Mrs. Mover is now moving closer toward Sharel.) "In the first part, you have to tell what you think just happened," answers Sharel. "That's right, and what do you think has just happened, Corey?" Corey replies, "I think she just found a puppy." Really? Does anyone disagree with that? "I do," says Tanner. "She didn't just find the puppy, because it says she found the puppy four years ago!" "That's correct," says Mrs. Mover.

Mrs. Mover now goes to one side of the room, where she uncovers a large display of the entire first paragraph. "OK, Corey, why don't you come on over here and give me a hand?" (Corey gladly proceeds to the display as Mrs. Mover sits in his desk. She now assumes the role of the student, and Corey assumes the role of the teacher.) "Corey, please use the yellow marker to highlight the first two sentences of the paragraph." All students watch as Corey obliges. "Now, Corey, please read us only the part that is highlighted." Corey reads, "It was a day Rachel would always remember, but would spend the rest of her life trying to forget. The memory of him lying there in his stillness would remain embedded in her vision forever." After Corey finishes reading, Mrs. Mover guides Corey and the others toward the correct answer to the first part of question 1. After much discussion, they finally all agree that what has just happened is that the dog has just been euthanized. Mrs. Mover gets the students to tell her—she could tell them, but that would not be nearly as effective—the evidence (the second part of the question): Rachel says that she would "spend the rest of her life trying to forget...him lying there in his stillness."

Note: Thus far, this activity has taken about 20 minutes, and they are still on the first paragraph. However, when they do move on—after more questioning, prodding, explaining, and discussing—Mrs. Mover will be certain that all of the students understand the storyline.

Mrs. Mover reads the first few pages of the story to the students while constantly walking in and out of the aisles, stopping for a while near any student whom she suspects of not being on task. Then she asks them all to pick apart, analyze, and answer several questions that require that the students use critical-thinking skills. (Mrs. Mover knew from the onset that many would unable to do that and would need much guidance and practice before becoming proficient at the skill.)

This particular short story was only six pages in length, yet Mrs. Mover used an entire week of class time on it. Here are some of the teaching techniques and activities that went along with the story:

- Teacher "read-alouds"
- Teacher-assisted question-and-answer sessions
- Student-to-student discussions
- Cooperative grouping exercises (Mrs. Mover joined the groups as needed)
- Hands-on activities to find the story elements
- Hands-on activities to answer critical-thinking questions
- Student-generated higher-order questions

Mrs. Mover used a variety of teaching methods and activities to teach all of the short stories in this unit. The class spent many hours deciphering, analyzing, answering, and discussing difficult story questions. Mrs. Mover knew that if she allowed the students to move forward before they grasped specific concepts, they would be lost. The only way she could possibly ascertain whether they were "getting it" was to be right in there with them the whole time! Mrs. Mover was unable to sit for even a minute during the entire unit because she knew that the students needed her constant assistance in order to succeed in their endeavor to read and respond correctly to the written word. By the time the final test was given at the end of the unit, the class average was a 90%, and the lowest score was an 81%. Wow!

What Doesn't Work

 Mrs. Stationary, like Mrs. Mover, studies the curriculum for the upcoming unit on "Reading and Responding to Literature." It is a six-week unit that concludes with a test requiring students to read passages from unfamiliar stories and then respond to critical-thinking questions. In other words, they must be able to read the material and comprehend, analyze, and apply what they have read. Her students' past test scores indicate that they are below average in their ability to read and respond to literature. Mrs. Stationary, who has very low expectations for her students, knows that the scores on this particular test will be low. "What do they expect me to do?" Mrs. Stationary asks herself. "Perform miracles?" Mrs. Stationary knows that most of these seventh-grade students are currently reading below grade level, yet, she thinks, "The school expects them to score well on a reading and responding test? These students don't do their homework; they don't do their class work; and they don't care about their grades! They are simply not teachable!"

Mrs. Stationary plans her lesson with the preconceived notion that her students are simply not teachable; therefore, the lesson that she plans is one in which she does not do much teaching! The following lesson is an example of what Mrs. Stationary's "Reading and Responding" unit covered:

- Class begins. Mrs. Stationary instructs the students to open their books to the story that they will read today.

- The students are instructed to read the story and answer the questions at the end of the story.

- The students hand in questions and answers at the end of class.

- Mrs. Stationary corrects the students' papers (during her next class) and returns them the following day. She goes over the questions and gives the students the correct answers. The students are instructed to begin reading the next story.

This lesson is repeated, day after day, for each story. There is no variation in teaching method, no differentiation of instruction, and no evidence that the teacher is accounting for differences in learning styles or other individual differences. There is no excitement, nor is there any teacher involvement. Unlike Mrs. Mover's lesson, Mrs. Stationary's lesson contains none of the following:

- ◆ Teacher "read-alouds"
- ◆ Teacher-assisted question-and-answer sessions
- ◆ Student-to-student discussions
- ◆ Cooperative grouping exercises
- ◆ Hands-on activities
- ◆ Student-generated higher-order questions

Mrs. Stationary is not actively involved with her students. She spends the majority of each class period far removed from them, sitting at her desk in the front corner of the classroom. Unfortunately, most of her verbal correspondence with her students comes in the form of reprimands. At the beginning of this chapter, you learned that Mrs. Stationary had referred 122 students to the office for disciplinary infractions in two years! After reading about her class, it is clear why her students are misbehaving:

- ◆ They are bored.
- ◆ They are unsuccessful.
- ◆ They are not being motivated or inspired.
- ◆ They are receiving no assistance.

Summary

 Physical barriers often create emotional barriers. Teachers who use physical barriers in their classrooms give the impression that they are not interested in bonding with their students. A teacher who is physically far removed from his or her students cannot effectively relate to them. If we want our students to engage in learning, we must not physically disengage ourselves from them.

Let's take one final look into these two classrooms...

Mrs. Mover

- ◆ She constantly moved around the room.
- ◆ She was always engaged with her students.
- ◆ She complimented her students often.
- ◆ She kept students on task by showing interest in their work.
- ◆ She used a variety of teaching methods to avoid monotony and boredom.

- She encouraged discussions in which she gently guided students toward the answer.

Mrs. Stationary

- She used her desk as a physical barrier between herself and her students.
- She was usually disengaged from her students.
- Because she failed to show interest, her students were often off task.
- She did not use a variety of teaching methods; therefore, her classes were monotonous and boring.

Because she was not engaged in the teaching and learning process, her students were not engaged in their class work. The students, however, did engage in other class activities, as evidenced by the 122 discipline referrals!

> ## I Heard What You Did
>
> *If I can just remember*
> *That my words are simply sounds*
> *That children hear in one ear and out*
> *Too often, I have found*
> *And more compared to what I do*
> *(Or less to be exact)*
> *For what I do is what they hear*
> *This matter is a fact*
> *Children watch our every move*
> *It's what we do, not say*
> *That children mimic every time*
> *The power's in the play.*
>
> Elizabeth Breaux
> *Classroom Management Simplified*

The Teacher as Role Model: They Hear What We Do

Children really do watch our every move—and by the way, so do adults! Words mean nothing if they are not reinforced by actions.

Whenever we choose to place ourselves in positions of authority, we choose to become role models.

- Parents are role models for their children.
- Store managers are role models for their employees.
- Surgeons are role models for their interns.
- Sergeants are role models for their troops.
- Principals are role models for their teachers.

♦ *Teachers are role models for their students (and for other teachers).*

Let's use parents as an example: Imagine parents who do not work to support their children financially but rely on other family members to do so. These parents spend little time with their children, and they are often verbally and physically abusive when they do. They use foul language as part of their daily vocabulary. They lie, cheat, and steal and often encourage the children to do the same. Through their actions, they are modeling all of the following:

- ♦ Verbal abuse
- ♦ Physical abuse
- ♦ Use of foul language
- ♦ Lying
- ♦ Cheating
- ♦ Stealing

As bystanders, we would expect these children to follow in their parents' footsteps. It's only natural because these children mimic what has been modeled for them.

The same rule applies in the classroom. We must be attuned to our every move, for our every move is being watched! Just imagine teachers who are poor role models. They might exhibit some of these characteristics:

- ♦ They are often late for work.
- ♦ They are disorganized and unprepared.
- ♦ They gossip about colleagues or students.
- ♦ They dress inappropriately or unprofessionally.
- ♦ They exhibit inappropriate use of spoken or written language.
- ♦ They treat students and other teachers disrespectfully.
- ♦ They engage in power struggles with students or other teachers.
- ♦ They lose paperwork.
- ♦ They lack the ability to follow through with necessary school-related tasks

Can you imagine any child behaving properly under these conditions? Can you imagine what will happen when these students begin mimicking the behaviors that are being modeled for them? Scary!

Situation

 A university is in the process of establishing Model Classrooms in its local public school district. Professors from the College of Education attend a monthly principals' meeting in the public school district so that they can address all of the school principals in one forum. The professors explain that they would like to establish a cross-section of Model Classrooms in which all grade levels and disciplines are represented. The professors would like the principals to present the plan to their faculties and encourage volunteers. The process for selecting teachers will involve an application, an interview, recommendations from administrators and fellow teachers, and five unannounced classroom observations (to be performed by the professors). The teachers who are selected will receive a handsome stipend for the extra time that they will be required to spend with the teacher interns. The professors ask that the principals emphasize the importance of the unannounced classroom observations. It is imperative that the teachers who are chosen are those who have proven themselves to be superb models at all times (because the students in the College of Education will be coming to observe at unannounced times).

Ms. Landor, the principal at one local high school, returns to her school and plans a faculty meeting. During the meeting, she presents the proposal that was submitted by the college professors. She explains to the teachers, "In the event that you are chosen, your classroom will become an open one—one where college students can enter without notice to observe you at any time. The application process is rigorous, as it should be. These future educators will be coming to see teaching at its finest. You must be models of that." She tells the teachers that before they even consider applying to be one of the Model Classroom teachers, they should do a complete inventory of themselves. She hands out a self-evaluation sheet and encourages all who intend to apply to complete it first.

Mrs. Brown is interested in applying. She is already a mentor teacher and truly enjoys working with and assisting new teachers. She has 27 years of experience and has been named Teacher of the Year six times during her career. Mrs. Brown is the kind of teacher we all remember when we recall our all-time favorite teacher:

- Enthusiastic
- Energetic
- Motivating
- Inspiring
- Kind
- Firm yet fair

- Knowledgeable
- Interesting
- Innovative

Mrs. Brown, like many of the education field's finest teachers, is always striving to become better. She often second-guesses her actions in the classroom, simply because she is constantly wondering whether she can be even better at her job. She reads the self-inventory list, which she has just received from Ms. Landor in the faculty meeting, and with some trepidation, she places a check mark next to each item. (See her list in the "What Works" section in this chapter.)

Ms. Hayes would also like to apply to be a Model Classroom teachers. She has been teaching for 17 years. Ms. Hayes is a teacher who has a lot of potential but seldom reaches it. She can always be counted on to do her share but little more. She is often late for school and for meetings, but she always has an excuse. She is capable of becoming a model teacher, but she does not always model what is best. Her inconsistencies would make her a poor candidate.

Both Ms. Hayes and Mrs. Brown complete the self-inventory given to them by their principal, Ms. Landor. Knowing that these will not be handed in to anyone, they complete them with honesty and candor. We'll take a look at Mrs. Brown's list in the "What Works" section and at Ms. Hayes' list in the "What Doesn't Work" section.

What Works

Mrs. Brown completed the self-evaluation and felt comfortable noting that all of the items on the list applied to her. She proceeded to apply for one of the positions by first obtaining the necessary references from her administrators and fellow teachers. (All references, of course, were testaments to her impeccable teaching skills.) She submitted the application and attended the interview. The professors were quite impressed, even more so once they completed their unannounced classroom observations. Mrs. Brown was definitely a candidate for the program. Mrs. Brown's self-evaluation looked like this:

Teacher Self-Evaluation

(Check all that apply to you. This is for the purposes of self-reflection and is not intended to be shared with anyone.)

✓ I am punctual and dependable.

✓ I have a gift for motivating students to reach and exceed their potential.

✓ I am enthusiastic and energetic.

✓ I am highly knowledgeable of the subject matter that I teach.

✓ I implement rules and procedures with consistency.

✓ I rarely refer students to the office.

✓ I teach from bell to bell every day.

✓ I differentiate my instruction to reach all students.

✓ I offer students many opportunities to earn points and grades.

✓ Rarely does a student fail my class.

✓ My students are very respectful of me and vice versa.

✓ I am always in search of ways to become a better teacher.

✓ I am comfortable being observed by anyone at any time.

In their observations of Mrs. Brown, the professors noted that all observed the following:

- Teacher punctuality/student punctuality
- Teacher enthusiasm/student enthusiasm
- Teacher highly involved/students all on task
- Teacher respectful of students/students respectful of teacher
- Teacher professionally dressed/students dressed according to dress code
- Teacher organized and prepared/students organized and prepared

The students were modeling Mrs. Brown to perfection!

NOTE: Mrs. Brown became a Model Classroom teacher, showing new teachers how to model for students precisely what you'd expect them to model for you in return!

What Doesn't Work

 Mrs. Hayes also completed the self-evaluation, using it as a very helpful self-reflection tool. She realized that she had more work to do before her classroom could be open as a model of impeccable teaching. She decided that she would apply anyway, knowing that the Model Classrooms program would not be open until the following year. She submitted the application and attended the interview. The professors were impressed, but their impressions changed after they observed her classroom. Mrs. Hayes still had some work to do, as reflected in her honest self-evaluation:

Teacher Self-Evaluation

(Check all that apply to you. This is for the purposes of self-reflection and is not intended to be shared with anyone.)

    I am punctual and dependable.

✓ I have a gift for motivating students to reach and exceed their potential.

    I am enthusiastic and energetic.

✓ I am highly knowledgeable of the subject matter that I teach.

    I implement rules and procedures with consistency.

    I rarely refer students to the office.

    I teach from bell to bell every day.

    I differentiate my instruction to reach all students.

✓ I offer students many opportunities to earn points and grades.

    Rarely does a student fail my class.

✓ My students are very respectful of me and vice versa.

✓ I am always in search of ways to become a better teacher.

    I am comfortable being observed by anyone at any time.

In their observations of Mrs. Hayes, the professors noted that all observed the following:

- Teacher tardiness/student tardiness
- Teacher disorganization/student disorganization
- Teacher lack of enthusiasm/student lack of enthusiasm

- Teacher disengaged from students/students disengaged and not on task

The students were modeling Mrs. Hayes to perfection!

Summary

Nowhere is the old saying "Actions speak louder than words" truer than it is in the classroom. We are models of everything that we do. It is only when our actions speak of our compassion and love for children that our students will begin to listen to our words. Shortcuts simply do not exist. Trying to find them is a sad waste of energy.

The fact is this: What I expect from my students, I must demonstrate first!

- I cannot expect them to respect me if I do not respect them.
- I cannot expect them to enjoy learning if I do not enjoy teaching them.
- I cannot expect loyalty from them if I am disloyal.
- I cannot expect them to stay on task if I am not joining them in the effort.

I am a model of all that I do. My students are watching, and they are "hearing" everything that they see.

Summary of Part I

Reaching students can be a daunting task, but it is an essential one nevertheless. At times, it can be overwhelming and disheartening. Have you ever wanted to simply throw your hands in the air and give up? If you haven't, you're probably a brand new teacher who has not yet graced the floors of a classroom!

Those of us who have been there know that it gets better every year because *we get better every year.* We truly become masters at reaching students, and then we are able to teach them, imparting the wealth of knowledge that we came here to divulge in the first place. Once you reach your students, you can truly teach them anything!

Let's take a quick look back at what the endeavor to reach students entails:

- I must make a *great first impression* on my students.
- I must believe in the *power of thanks and praise.*
- I must be *assertive and in-control* at all times.
- I must learn to *implement procedures to perfection,* or my students will implement their own procedures in their own ways.
- I must be utterly consistent when *enforcing consequences* and create an environment in which students know the *ifs* and *thens.*
- I must *make home contacts* early and often to form an alliance with my students' parents and to ensure that they are on my side.
- I must refuse to negotiate in nonnegotiable situations in order to *avoid power struggles* with my students.
- I must be a *mobile teacher* who realizes the significance of being everywhere.
- I must understand and believe that students truly *hear what I do* and that I am a *role model* for my students.

You must believe in yourself and know that you have the power to make a difference in your classroom each and every day. You have the power and the tools to reach your students. No one can do that for you. You cannot be beaten down unless you choose to be. You alone will make the choices—*please choose wisely.*

How to
Teach All Students

If I Could Teach My Students

If I could teach my students one solitary thing
A sense of ever questioning to each child I would bring
And by their curiosity, they'd learn to teach themselves
For the more that one uncovers, the deeper that he delves
If as one student's teacher, I light a fire within
Then I have touched the world indeed—influence does not end.

Annette Breaux
Real Teachers, Real Challenges, Real Solutions

> **If I Survive**
>
> *I'm certain that I placed it there*
> *I'm looking for it everywhere*
> *Behind the doors and under chairs*
> *Beneath the floor and in the air.*
>
> *One day I will get organized*
> *Next year sounds good (if I survive)*
> *A better plan I must contrive*
> *I'll do it tomorrow, if I'm alive!*
>
> Elizabeth Breaux
> *Classroom Management Simplified*

The Well-Organized Classroom: Like Teacher, Like Students

OK, I'll admit it—I am an organized person! I cringe at the mere thought of disorganization. My blood pressure skyrockets when I enter a classroom that is disorganized. Because of my work with teachers, I am in and out of many classrooms, and I can tell you without reservation that a cluttered, messy, disorganized classroom environment is a chaotic environment that is reflective of fragmented, disjointed teaching and learning. They go hand in hand.

I'm certainly not saying that disorganized teachers are not (or do not have the potential to be) good teachers. What I am saying is that if these good teachers became better organized, they'd be *better* teachers!

Even those of us who consider ourselves to be organized people sometimes slip a little. You know what I'm talking about.

- We allow the back seat of our car to become a little cluttered.

- We let our closet at home become a little overcrowded and messy.

- We push the old food in the refrigerator to the back to accommodate fresh food.

- We jam the mess into the bedroom closet and close the door to give the appearance of organization.

- We have to rent a dump truck at the end of the school year to haul away the bags of trash we fill after cleaning up the classroom in preparation for the next year!

We've all been there. We've all had those "clean up and get organized days." And how good did it feel once everything was organized again? It feels good because we always function better in the midst of organization. When we free ourselves of physical clutter, we free ourselves of mental clutter as well. If this were not the case, millions of dollars would not be handed over to publishing companies every year for books and videos on the topic of "organizing everything from your garage to your bathroom"! In this hectic day of working mothers and working fathers, we realize that becoming organized in all that we do (both at work and at home) will help us free up more quality time for our families.

The same is true for the classroom, where even the best teachers become better when they become better organized and are able to use their time more efficiently and effectively for teaching. I hear teachers complain all the time about not having enough time to teach all that is expected. This is so true, especially in this day and age of high-stakes testing. It only stands to reason, however, that if two teachers are to teach the same curriculum in the same amount of time, the one who is highly organized (and thus experiences no lost class time because of disorganization) can be more efficient and effective than the teacher who is disorganized and loses precious minutes as a result of disorganization.

If you are a teacher who is already fairly organized but wants to become even better organized, or if you are a teacher who has finally hit rock bottom and is searching for a way out of the pit, these tips for becoming organized might help.[1]

---

1 See Elizabeth Breaux, *Classroom Management Simplified* (Larchmont, NY: Eye on Education, 2005.)

Tips for Becoming Organized

- Determine the amount of physical space you have and how that space can be best organized for maximum efficiency.

- Arrange your own personal space first. Remember, you live there!

- Create rooms and stations within your classroom.

- Color code everything!

- Create bins for everything! Bins should be clearly labeled.

- Create and display charts for everything—for example, conduct chart, extra points chart, and tardy chart. Make certain to assign numbers to students. Names should never be written on the charts.

- Label or color code shelves and cubbyholes by class (if you teach more than one class) and then by material. Students will know what is off limits to them and what is not. They also know where items "live" in the classroom.

- Create supply boxes for your students. Fill a small plastic box with the necessary classroom supplies (pens, pencils, scissors, glue, ruler, eraser, crayons, compass, protractor, highlighter, calculator). Place one in each desk. Write the name of every student who sits in that desk (if you teach more than one class) on the box. When students arrive, familiarize them with the supply boxes. Tell them that they are responsible for checking the box daily and telling the teacher immediately if they notice that something is missing. This, of course, means that the student in the last class "accidentally" left with something that belongs in the box. The teacher can then retrieve the missing item. (The teacher will be reimbursed for the cost of the supplies because the students' supply lists include all or most of the items in the boxes. As students bring in their supplies, the teacher can collect and stockpile items as replacements for the remainder of the year. There are usually enough supplies left over at the end of the year to create boxes for the next year.)

- Assign one student per row or group to be the materials supervisor and show these students where everything "lives" in your classroom.

- Determine a space or place for everything. Don't deviate. If an item is taken from its place, it must be returned to its place, no questions asked!

Situation

A review of test data from the previous school year shows that a large discrepancy between the eighth-grade math classes of Mrs. Array and Mrs. Disarray. Mrs. Array's students demonstrated an overall class average of 91%, whereas Mrs. Disarray's students achieved an overall class average of 76%. The new principal, Mrs. McCarley, is quite concerned about Mrs. Disarray's classes and wants to determine the underlying causes. A repeat of the previous year is not acceptable.

Principal McCarley begins her quest to discover the underlying causes by scheduling frequent observations of both classroom teachers. During the first few (unannounced) visits, Principal McCarley simply observes and takes notes. During each subsequent visit, she reflects on the previous observation to determine which practices (both positive and negative) are ongoing. After several observations, Principal McCarley combines all of her notes into one document. She makes a list of pros and cons for each teacher. After studying and comparing the lists, Principal McCarley need not look any further. She can see the reason for the difference in student achievement between the two classes.

What Works

Every visit to Mrs. Array's room was an adventure and a learning experience. Principal McCarley watched, listened, learned, and took notes. She observed not only the teaching but also the physical arrangement of the room. She noticed that there was a specific place for everything, and everything was in its place. Many items were used frequently, but the students always made certain to properly replace everything that was used. Rules and procedures were obviously in place. Had they not been in place, a very different learning environment would have existed.

Principal McCarley was amazed at the impeccable utilization of time. Mrs. Array seemed to be able to fit more into one class period than anyone she'd ever seen. It took only one visit before Principal McCarley uncovered the secret. It was really no secret at all—Mrs. Array was simply very well organized. The physical organization of the room, coupled with Mrs. Array's meticulous planning, allowed her to efficiently cover a greater amount of material in less time.

After several visits, Principal McCarley sat down to create a list of pros and cons for Mrs. Array's performance. After completing the list of pros, Principal McCarley decided that creating a list of cons would be a waste of time. There simply seemed to be no cons.

Teacher: Mrs. Array

Pros

- Mrs. Array greets students at the door, closes the door, and begins class. There is no wasted time.

- Information for students is kept on a chart wall, where the students' names are replaced by numbers. Students can find personal information regarding tardiness, conduct, homework, and absences, but they are not privy to information regarding other students (because names are not used).

- The room is well arranged and organized for effective teaching. Mrs. Array teaches five different groups of students, and all items are arranged according to color. She and the students use bins, charts, supply bags, class folders, and class portfolios, and all are color coded red, blue, green, yellow, or orange. Classes are allowed to use only the items that bear their class's color.

- Mrs. Array seems to love activities that involve hands-on work. Items are available and ready to go daily. No time is wasted because of lack of preparation.

- Group work runs beautifully. Mrs. Array has obviously put much time into teaching students cooperative grouping strategies and etiquette. Therefore, no time is wasted during group work.

- Mrs. Array moves from one activity to the next by going through three steps:

  1. She stops all students.

  2. She gives them 30 seconds to pick up all materials.

  3. She gives them 30 seconds to prepare for the next activity.

     Note: Anyone not meeting the time line loses points on the daily rubric.

- Mrs. Array uses a hand signal to gain students' attention. It is immediate and without flaw. There is no whining, begging, pleading, or negotiating, and there is no lost class time.

- Mrs. Array's roll book is beautiful. It is neat, easy to read, loaded with grades, up to date, and accurate.

- Mrs. Array has what she calls the "Homework Hotline," where students drop homework into a bin as they enter the classroom. Mrs. Array checks the bin while students are working on an activity, then makes a list of home phone numbers of students whose homework is missing. Her students all seem to do their homework! (Upon further investigation, it was found that Mrs. Array calls parents when homework is not completed. She obviously has been consistent with the home calls because most students turn in their homework.)

- The room is neat, clean, and free of trash. Students clean their personal spaces before dismissal. All class materials are returned to their proper holding places.

- Mrs. Array allows the row that has completed all end-of-period tasks to leave first, and then others follow in order of readiness.

- Mrs. Array follows the last row out of the room and then awaits her next class. She has no cleaning up to do. The students have done it for her!

- Mrs. Array is interesting, well planned, innovative, and hardworking. She is kind to her students yet firm in her implementation of rules and procedures. She is respectful to her students and respected by her students.

What Doesn't Work

 Just as each visit to Mrs. Array's room was a learning experience for Principal McCarley, so was each visit to Mrs. Disarray's room. Needless to say, the experiences were quite different, as Principal McCarley had expected (based on the huge discrepancy in test scores). Principal McCarley watched, listened, learned, and took notes, just as she did in Mrs. Array's room. She observed not only the teaching but also the physical arrangement of the room. She noticed that the room appeared messy, cluttered, and disorganized. This physical appearance was reflected in the teaching practices. Mrs. Disarray never seemed to be able to find the necessary teaching materials that she needed. On two separate occasions, she sent a student to the office to copy a handout that was needed for class, one that she had neglected to run off herself.

Rules and procedures were obviously not in place because the chaos was immensely evident. (Rules and procedures are always evident when they are *not* in place. That's when you see the chaos and the disorganization that is caused by their absence!)

Principal McCarley was amazed at the amount of downtime in Mrs. Disarray's classroom. Time was lost at the beginning of the period when students were allowed to enter late without consequence. No organized plan for turning in homework existed, so this task always took much longer than necessary. There were no holding bins for materials, so many materials that Mrs. Disarray intended for the students to use always seemed to be lost (or taken). Transitions from one activity to the next were an obliteration of useful time.

This lack of organization caused a severe deficiency in time management that had already caused this class to fall far behind Mrs. Array's class, and it was only the second week of school!

Once again, Principal McCarley devised a list of pros and cons. Unfortunately, Mrs. Disarray's list of pros was short. Sadly, Principal McCarley had a difficult time finding anything at all to note that was positive. Principal McCarley did realize, however, that the problems were fixable and that once fixed, the great teacher inside Mrs. Disarray would be able to emerge.

Teacher: Mrs. Disarray

Cons

- Mrs. Disarray does not greet students; instead, she is busy trying to clean up the mess left by the previous class.

- Students enter late and without consequence. Therefore, precious minutes are immediately forfeited.

- The room is unkempt, untidy, messy, and disorganized.

- Hands-on activities, although terrific teaching and learning methods in theory, are ruined in practice. A lack of organization leads to chaos, confusion, and wasted time.

- Mrs. Disarray appears ill planned for the day's lesson and wastes much time on improvisation. The lesson becomes fragmented and objectives cannot be met.

- Mrs. Disarray has no procedure in place for gaining the attention of her students; therefore, she wastes precious time begging, pleading, and negotiating with the students.

- Mrs. Array's roll book is incomplete, out of order, and lacks a sufficient amount of grades for each student.

- Mrs. Disarray allows the bell to dismiss her class. Students leave without putting away class materials. Trash is left in and on desks.

Summary

If we free ourselves of physical clutter, we free ourselves of mental clutter. Organization breeds orderliness, and orderliness opens the door to effective teaching and learning. Without organization and order, we cannot be nearly as effective as we could be with them. An organized environment is a breeding ground for learning.

Learning simply cannot take place in a chaotic, disorganized environment. If we as teachers are disorganized, we will not be able to command organization from our students. Within Mrs. Disarray, there probably lies a highly effective, highly knowledgeable teacher hidden beneath the disorganization and chaos. She just needs to get organized, allowing the best teacher within her to emerge and grow.

Remember the modeling philosophy? *They hear what we do.* Mrs. Array was a model of organization. Mrs. Disarray was a model of disorganization. Mrs. Array's students functioned in an organized manner. Mrs. Disarray's students were disorderly and disorganized. The final proof was in the test scores: Mrs. Array, 91% class average, Mrs. Disarray, 76% class average.

The Lesson

She gets right down to business
She doesn't waste a minute
She tells us what her plan is
And assures that we are in it.

She tells us quite precisely
What she'll teach us to do
She usually tells a story
That relates to something new.

She shows us how it should be done
We watch her so intently
Then with her help we try it
(She mends mistakes, but gently).

She helps us do it once again
Or twice, or thrice, or more
Then when we finally get it right
She still has more in store.

She says she thinks we're ready
To try it on our own
(Although she steps aside this time
We're never all alone).

The bell is just about to ring
Class is almost through
"Five minutes left," she says to us
"Time for a quick review."

Elizabeth Breaux

Effective Instruction: What Does It Really Look Like?

What is effective instruction? What does it look like? If students leave the classroom at the end of the period without the benefit of new knowledge, did effective instruction take place? I would think not. Effective instruction takes many shapes and forms, but the bottom line is that in its presence, teaching and learning occur. A transfer of knowledge from teacher to student must occur or else learning cannot.

Think of all the things that go on in your own classroom from day to day. How many of those activities, teaching methods, and strategies are eliciting learning? Are you certain that on every class day—every single one— your students are learning something new? Upon leaving your classroom, do your students possess knowledge that they did not have when they entered?

Let's do a quick inventory of some of the day-to-day teaching practices that occur in the typical classroom. Which ones would you consider effective *teaching* practices?

- The teacher lectures.
- The students take notes during a lecture.
- The students copy notes from the board.
- The teacher gives the students notes on an upcoming chapter.
- The teacher gives an overview of the upcoming chapter, tells a story that relates to the upcoming chapter, completes the chapter (with the students), and then gives notes on the chapter.
- The students read a chapter silently.
- The students answer questions at the end of a chapter (independently).
- The teacher relates an upcoming activity to a real-life experience.
- The teacher reads aloud and initiates a discussion about the meaning of an unfamiliar word. Once the discussion is over, students look up the word in the dictionary to determine which definition is correct.
- The teacher gives the students 10 unfamiliar vocabulary words in isolation (no context). They look up the words in the dictionary and copy them into their notebooks.
- The students independently complete a packet of worksheets.
- The students take a written test.
- The students work in cooperative groups with teacher guidance and assistance. A rubric is used for assessment, and students are graded at various points throughout the activity.

Before you read on, determine which practices you feel are effective *teaching* methods. (The key word is *teaching*!) This is not to say that any or all of these practices cannot to be used in isolation, but some are obviously not good methods of instruction because no teaching is going on.

During a recent inservice session, teachers examined and discussed this list. The general consensus was that the following teaching practices and methods are effective (shown with a check mark):

The teacher lectures.

The students take notes during a lecture.

The students copy notes from the board.

The teacher gives the students notes on an upcoming chapter.

✓ The teacher gives an overview of the upcoming chapter, tells a story that relates to the upcoming chapter, completes the chapter (with the students), and then gives notes on the chapter.

The students read a chapter silently.

The students answer questions at the end of a chapter (independently).

✓ The teacher relates an upcoming activity to a real-life experience.

✓ The teacher reads aloud and initiates a discussion about the meaning of an unfamiliar word. Once the discussion is over, students look up the word in the dictionary to determine which definition is correct.

The teacher gives the students 10 unfamiliar vocabulary words in isolation (no context). They look up the words in the dictionary and copy them into their notebooks.

The students independently complete a packet of worksheets.

The students take a written test.

✓ The students work in cooperative groups with teacher guidance and assistance. A rubric is used for assessment, and students are graded at various points throughout the activity.

During the discussion, the general feelings of the teachers were as follows:

◆ Lecture is monotonous, boring, and uneventful. Students quickly lose interest, making it extremely difficult for learning to occur.

◆ Without previous knowledge, students have nothing to which they can relate the notes they are given; therefore, note taking that precedes discussion is meaningless.

- Reading teachers who typically assign students to read a chapter and then answer end-of-chapter questions are not teaching the students how to read. (No one was opposed to silent, sustained reading in general, however; it certainly has its place.)

- The old "vocabulary days" should be history! (The term refers to the days when teachers assigned 25 words per week. Students were to define the words using a dictionary, copy the definitions into their notebooks, and memorize the definitions for Friday's test.)

- Effective teaching cannot take place when students are busy completing worksheet after worksheet, especially when there is no teacher guidance, assistance, checking, discussion, and rechecking. No one was opposed to worksheets as extra practice or supplemental teaching devices, because they are one way to tell whether the students understand what has just been taught. They should be used sporadically, though. Sometimes just a section or two is a sufficient indicator of whether the students have learned the material.

- When students are being tested, no teaching is occurring. Students still must be assessed, but the assessment should be quick so that teaching can continue!

Situation

 A group of interns from a local university are completing their internships at a local middle school. The university and the school have partnered, and the interns have been assigned only to this school. Instead of being assigned to a particular teacher, they have been assigned to a team of teachers (usually four to five). As a result, they will receive the benefit of observing and teaching in different settings and disciplines.

As is typical with all (or most) teachers, we share what we see! After one week of observations, two of the interns were having lunch in the teachers' lounge. In the next section, read how their conversation transpired.

What Works (Intern 1) and What Doesn't Work (Intern 2)

Intern 1: "Have you been in Mr. Lewis's class yet? It's amazing! He makes it look so easy. And the kids are so well behaved in there. I can't figure out why."

Intern 2: "Well, I've been in Mr. Todd's class, and I certainly can't say the same. Mr. Todd has some really bad kids, though. You just wouldn't believe some of the things they do in there."

Intern 1: "But Mr. Todd and Mr. Lewis are on the same team, which means they teach the same kids."

Intern 2: "That's right. I hadn't thought about that. Tell me about Mr. Lewis's class, and I'll tell you about Mr. Todd's class. We're going to be switching teachers next week anyway, so I'll soon see for myself."

Intern 1: "Well, Mr. Lewis seems so nice. The students love him and he really seems to love them. He doesn't let them get away with anything, and they know it. In fact, the students work from bell to bell every day and don't seem to mind at all."

Intern 2: "Are you sure that Mr. Lewis and Mr. Todd are on the same team? The students that you are describing *do not* sound like the ones I see in Mr. Todd's class."

Intern 1: "I'm sure. They definitely are the same ones. Are Yvette Brown and Christy Hayes in one of the classes?"

Intern 2: "Yes! They are so bad. They are always in trouble. You wouldn't believe some of the things they do in Mr. Todd's class. They glued a student to his seat the other day. I think that what happened is that when the student got up, they put glue in the seat of his desk. He came back and sat down, and the kids just laughed and laughed for the rest of the period (most of us didn't know why they were laughing), and the poor student didn't even realize that he was glued down and wasn't going anywhere. He did finally realize it when the bell rang and he tried to get up. It was a little late by then, because they had used that new cement glue. Mr. Todd later told me that he and the custodian had to cut him out of his shorts to release him. Mr. Todd finally found out who did it, and now Yvette and Christy are both suspended from school."

Intern 1: "I cannot believe that. Those two *never* cause trouble in Mr. Lewis's class. Now that I think about it, they don't have time to cause trouble. Mr. Lewis keeps them far too busy. And I'm not kidding. Class starts when the bell rings. The first thing Mr. Lewis does is what he calls his 'Focus.' He directs them to something in the room that is an attention grabber. It's always different, so the students never know what to expect. It's actually kind of exciting. He usually relates it to something they have already done, and then he tells them what they will be able to do by the end of the lesson. He's really stating the objectives, but in an innovative sort of way, I guess. Whatever he's doing, it works!"

Intern 2: "Well, if Mr. Todd were to state his objectives, I don't know what he would say. It seems to me that all he really wants for his students to be able to do is be quiet and complete their work while he sits at his desk and does something else. Maybe that's why the students are always in trouble."

Intern 1 "Mr. Lewis is not like that at all. He is right in there with his students for the entire period. Come to think of it, I don't think there is a chair behind his desk."

Intern 2: "Maybe he gave his chair to Mr. Todd. He sits so much he'll need a new one when the old one wears out!"

Intern 1: [Laughing] "That's not very nice."

Intern 2: [Laughing] "I know, but it's true."

Intern 1: "Well, with the lessons that Mr. Lewis presents to his students, they really need him. He always shows them how to do whatever it is that he is teaching them. Sometimes he shows them three or four times before they understand. He's very patient with the students, and they seem to appreciate that. He asks a lot of questions and makes certain every student is involved and understands before he moves on. He seems to like to allow them to work in groups. They do that almost every day."

Intern 2: "Groups? Those students know how to work in groups? Are you kidding me? I'm trying to imagine it now! The headlines would read: 'Group A glues Group B to the wall in Mr. Todd's class. Construction crews are working around the clock to release the affected students!'"

Intern 1: "Not only do they work in groups, but they work really well. They seem to know exactly what to do. (Mr. Lewis must have trained them well.) They get into groups quickly—I think he times them and gives extra points on the grading rubric just for that—and they get to work. Everyone seems to have a different job, and they keep one another on task. Mr. Lewis scuttles from group to group, assisting the students. They all seem to want him at once. I think they love his approval so much that they all want him to be close enough that he can see what they are doing."

Intern 2: "Maybe if Mr. Todd would do a little 'scuttling,' the students would not be able to get into so much trouble. The truth is, they are getting into trouble because they are bored. When you think about it, gluing someone to a desk is creative. I wouldn't advocate it, but it shows that the students' minds are working. Maybe if Mr. Todd were a little more creative with his lessons, the students wouldn't have to create their own activities and get into trouble."

Intern 1: "Just wait until you see these same students in Mr. Lewis's class. You won't believe it. Not only would they *never* glue a student to a desk, but they wouldn't even consider ruining a desk with glue! A few minutes before class ends, Mr. Lewis always leads a discussion in which he and the students review the lesson. They talk about what they've learned and how they will take it a step further in tomorrow's lesson. Then, he has them return the room to the order it was in when they arrived. Desks are put back in the correct places, class materials are returned, and the room is ready for the next class. It's beautiful. I hope I'm lucky enough to get these kinds of students when I get my own classroom."

Intern 2: "You'd just better pray that you don't get the ones that Mr. Todd has, or you'll be in big trouble."

Intern 1: "But aren't they the same students?"

Intern 2: "You're right. They are!"

Summary

 Let's take a final look at what effective instruction really looks like. We know that it can take many shapes and forms, but the outcome is always the same: *In the presence of effective instruction, teaching and learning take place.* If a teaching method does not require much teaching and does not elicit learning, it is not effective. If students don't need the teacher's assistance and guidance, then they probably have already perfected the particular skill and should move on.

Each day, students should leave the classroom with new knowledge. If that does not happen, they have not been taught. If the teacher is not teaching, the students are not learning.

Teaching does not always entail teacher-directed instruction, however. In Mr. Lewis's classroom, for example, the teacher did initially direct the instruction but insisted on student input and discussion. During the cooperative grouping activity, students directed the instruction with Mr. Lewis's assistance. There are many forms of effective instruction, and the best teachers use as many as possible. That's why their classes are interesting, highly active, and student oriented and the students are well behaved!

Final word: Student achievement results are indicators of both student achievement and teacher effectiveness. Teachers should use student achievement results to gauge their teaching success and to make necessary changes to their teaching practices.

Provide Some Inspiration

My teacher says I'll need this stuff
When I'm a little older
(I'd tell her I don't care right now
If only I were bolder)
Geometry and Algebra
History, Science, English
Just how it all pertains to me
I'm trying to distinguish.

Don't tell me that I'll need this
When I am an adult
What you don't seem to realize
Is that's a blunt insult
For I'm not an adult yet
I just cannot relate
To something that has never
Been placed upon my plate.

So if you want my interest
And my motivation
Then match it to my life today
Provide some inspiration
And once I understand
How I can use these things today
You won't believe the knowledge
You'll be able to relay!

Elizabeth Breaux

Real-Life Teaching Strategies: Make It Real and They Will Come!

For something to be real to us, it must have happened to us or affected us in some way. At the very least, we must be able to create some relationship to it for it to seem authentic. If something is real, it is

- ◆ Actual
- ◆ Authentic
- ◆ Bona fide
- ◆ Existent
- ◆ Factual

In other words, we give it merit or credence as being important. We willingly bring it into our consciousness as something that we can use in some way.

On the other hand, if we do not view something as being important or valid in our lives, we may reject it as immaterial. Many things affect our day-to-day survival. Those things are extremely important or real to us. A myriad of things exists that we consider important in the global sense, yet we do not embrace those things as being important to us at the particular time.

Let's make this a little clearer: If we assume that you are, have been, or will be a teacher, the concept of a "teacher retirement plan" will be important or real to you at some point in your life. Your proximity to retirement, however, will dictate just how important or real it is to you at any given time. Let's look at this example:

It's Friday afternoon and the bell is about to ring. Your weekend is about to begin. It's been a long week, and the dismissal bell is your best friend. "Please excuse the interruption," the principal chimes in, "But I have a *very important* announcement to make. I have just received word from the school board office that the state's teacher retirement system has been completely revamped. The overhaul is a drastic one that will affect us severely. State department personnel will be at the school board office at 4:00 this afternoon to present the new plan and answer any questions."

Question: Are you going to the meeting?

Answer: Probably not, unless you are about to retire.

I recently spoke to a faculty of about 100 teachers, and I posed the same question to them. Only six of them raised their hands when asked whether they would attend the meeting. A brief discussion revealed that all six were about to retire. This meeting was very real to them because the information could significantly affect their lives. The next questions I asked were directed at the participants who had not raised their hands. I first asked how many of them planned to make teaching a career. Almost every hand in the building went up. "That is proof," I said, "that retirement will eventually affect all of you. So why aren't you going to today's meeting?" The general consensus was that the effect was too far in the future for them to care much about the new retirement plan right now. "I've only been teaching for a few years," some said. "By the time I retire, the retirement plan will have changed several more times." "So," I said, "It sounds like you are saying that it's just not all that real to you right now."

Students in our classrooms view the materials that we teach in much the same manner. Our problem as teachers is that we already know how the material will affect their future lives because we've experienced the effects. We have to remember, though, that our students have not yet had the life experiences we have had. Therefore, we must find ways to make the material relevant to their lives today!

Is there anything more infuriating than planning what you think is a very good lesson, only to have students ask the exasperating question, "Why do we have to know this?" You know what I'm talking about. We've all been asked the question and felt the rage inside of us emerging. Stop! Don't say it—or you'll probably regret it. Instead, try to look at the question as a red flag that you have neglected to make a real-life connection between the material and the students' lives. Often, however, we do answer the question. Our answers are similar to these:

- You have to know this because you are going to have a family one day, and you will have to be able to pay bills, balance a checkbook, and run your household.
- You have to know this for high school next year.

If you look closely at these typical answers, you'll see that neither is real for the students at that moment. The children have not yet had a family and a household to run, nor have they attended high school, so these situations are not yet real to them.

We'll look at some examples of how to bring material to life in the next section. But first, let's look at some tips for making lessons real for your students.

Tips for Making Lessons Real

- Remember that you are the teacher. The supplemental materials—textbook, workbooks, programs—are only tools. They will only come to life when you make them real.

- Before beginning a lesson—any lesson—relate it to real life, but make sure it is the students' real life (past, present, or foreseeable future).

- Tell your students stories they can relate to. It may be a story about something that happened to another student, to you, or to someone they don't know. If they can relate to it in some way, you've got 'em!

- Allow students to make connections between the text and their own lives, a previously read text, and the world.

- Use hands-on activities as much as possible. Students respond better when they are able to manipulate something. On-task behavior will improve dramatically.

- Take them on field trips. Even a trip around the campus that relates to an aspect of your lesson can be immensely effective.

- Start looking at how you taught things to your own children, and model your lessons in that way. The truth is that in real life, we don't need a textbook, handbook, or worksheet. We get in there and we do it!

- Use the text as a vehicle for experience! For example, teach a history lesson through an English lesson, a math lesson through and industrial arts lesson, or a social studies lesson through a physical education lesson.

Unfortunately, many traditional methods of teaching do not elicit a real-life feeling or response; therefore, these methods are not engaging. The following are examples of traditional methods that, if used sparingly and properly, can have a place in the classroom.[1] Remember, however, that they can also be turn-offs when they are used as daily, ongoing instructional tools. (Caution: Lecture and storytelling are not synonymous!)

---

1 See Elizabeth Breaux, *Classroom Management Simplified* (Larchmont, NY: Eye on Education, 2005.)

Lecture: This is still one of the most often-used teaching methods, even though it is extremely ineffective. Think about teachers you had who stood in the front of the classroom, often behind a podium or desk, and talked in a monotonous, mundane, unenthusiastic manner for hours on end. How interested were you? How much did you learn? How much would you have paid to avoid that classroom each day?

> I remember a teacher who loved to talk *to* us as opposed to *at* us. She had a way of telling a story that related everything to our own lives in some way. She made certain that all of the students were able to share their own experiences throughout the lesson. We created things, both literally and figuratively, that gave meaning to the lesson. Yes, she talked *to* us a lot, but she never lectured *at* us!

Note taking: Don't get me wrong. I'm not opposed to students jotting down notes from time to time, as long as those notes have meaning that is based on prior knowledge. (In fact, there are some very effective, highly engaging note-taking strategies.) However, I am opposed to note taking in the absence of teaching or before the material has been introduced.

> Consider an effective note-taking scenario in which the teacher teaches a history lesson through storytelling. The characters and historical figures in the story are related to the students' own lives in some way. After the students have an understanding of the historical events, asking them to take notes can give meaning to the note taking. Students have already made sense of what is being written, so the note taking is not just another meaningless, time-consuming task.

Remember the class in which you walked in and the teacher had several pages of notes for you to copy? (I believe the teacher even called it a "study guide.") You spent hours taking notes and then even more hours studying notes that had no meaning because the material was never actually taught to you. You remember, the same teacher who said that "Kids today fail because they don't study!" Where's the teaching? (How would you like to go to a workshop or seminar at which the speaker gives you pages of notes to copy and study?)

Silent reading with little or no guidance: Before you throw this book against the nearest wall, let me assure you that I am certainly not opposed to reading! In fact, I was a language arts teacher. I love to read, and I love to see my students engaged in a good book. But, like you, I remember the teacher who said, "Open your book to page 30, read the story, and then answer the questions at the end of the story!"

> On the other hand, I also remember a teacher who actually taught while the story was being read. Sure, we read silently or aloud in groups, but we learned about story elements through discussions along the way. We learned our vocabulary by stopping at unfamiliar words and using context clues or other real-life strategies to determine the meaning. We also used a dictionary, but not until we had used context clues and discussion. We compared the story to events in our own lives or to a previously read story. We learned about characterization and stopped midway to write a character sketch. It may have taken us an entire week to read that story, but we learned so much along the way!

Worksheets: I am not opposed to worksheets, as long as they are used sparingly. Remember that a worksheet is used for one of two reasons: as a mini-assessment of what has been taught or as extra practice or reinforcement of what has been taught. We all remember a teacher who monopolized the copy machine copying stacks of worksheets every week. The one who gave you a packet of worksheets (busywork) almost every day. The one who sat at her desk grading yesterday's packet of worksheets while you worked on today's worksheets. The one who had tomorrow's packet of worksheets ready for today's early finishers.

Situation

 In this chapter, we'll look into the classrooms of several teachers, all of whom face the same challenges. All of them want to be able to motivate and inspire their students. All of them want their students to yearn for knowledge. All of them want their students to engage in daily lessons. Some of them realize that they must create an environment in which this can occur. The others keep hoping that it will happen on its own—yeah, right!

We'll look at some examples of what works and what doesn't work taken from the daily lessons of these teachers.

What Works

Example 1

Mrs. Ivy is a new second-grade teacher. After observing her students during the first few days of school, she is appalled at their table etiquette. She cannot believe how some eat with their hands, eat with their mouths wide open, touch others' food, rarely use napkins, and leave food on the tables. A plan has just occurred to her: As she is about to begin a lesson on fractions, she will teach both fractions and table manners in the same lesson. She will make it real to them, and they will grasp both concepts at once. She rushes to the store to buy supplies for the lesson: individually wrapped snack cakes, napkins, paper plates, plastic forks and knives, paper cups, and juice.

Mrs. Ivy arrives early at school the next morning. She sets the table at each student's desk. When the students arrive, she instructs them, "Go directly to your desks and sit quietly. You will notice that you all have cake and juice. You may not eat or drink it now, but you will be able to do so later. What I would like you to do right now is place your napkin in your lap." (The students are extremely excited and engaged and follow her directions explicitly.)

"Now, I would like all of you to look at me and watch what I am going to do." (All eyes are on Mrs. Ivy as she draws a circle on the board.) "This circle represents the cake that you have on your desk. I would like you to watch me and tell me what I am doing." (Mrs. Ivy, using her own knife, pretends to cut the cake in half by passing the knife straight down the center of the cake that she has drawn on the board.) "What did you see me do?" asks Mrs. Ivy. "You cut it in half," answers a student." "That's correct!"

"Now I would like those of you who are right-handed to hold your knife in your right hand and those of you who are left-handed to hold your knife in your left hand." (All of the students follow her directions.) "Now, pick up your fork and hold it in the other hand." (Mrs. Ivy is demonstrating with her own fork, knife, and cake.) "I would like you to stick the fork into the cake so that you can hold it down and, using your knife, cut the cake in half." (All of the students do this.) "Now, place your fork here (she shows them where it should be placed) and your knife here (again she shows them proper placement). Please look back up here. How many pieces of cake did I have before I cut it?" "Only one," answers a student. "And how many did I have after I cut it down the middle?" "Two," answers another student. "If I take one of those two new pieces away, how much of the cake will I have?" "One half," answers another student. "Very good," says Mrs. Ivy, as she writes "1/2" on the board next to the drawing of the cake.

"Now I would like you to cut your cake again, but this time I want you to cut it across." (She again demonstrates for the students as they follow her lead.) "How many pieces of cake do you have now?" "Four," says a student. "Notice that your cake is still one whole cake, but it is now cut into four pieces that we call 'fourths.'" (Mrs. Ivy writes "4/4" on the board to show that they now have four fourths, which, she explains, is the same as the whole.)

This lesson continues, with more discussion of fractions. There is absolutely no discussion of table manners (yet). Once Mrs. Ivy is ready to allow the students to eat their cake, she begins to review how they should place their napkins in their laps and use their utensils. She then says to the students, "We are about to eat our cake and drink our juice, but before we do so, let's review our table manners." She asks questions such as

- Where does your napkin go?
- How do you hold your knife and fork?
- Where do you place your knife when it is not being used?
- Should you ever eat with your mouth open?
- Is it proper to touch someone else's food? Why not?
- What should you do with your dishes and utensils once you are finished?
- What should you do if you accidentally drop crumbs on the floor or on your desk?

Once the discussion is over, she allows them to eat. She watches and assists, making certain that all use proper etiquette. Just before lunch that day, she reviews the lesson with her students and reminds them to remember what they have learned about good manners and to use them in the cafeteria. She assures them that she will be there to watch and remind them (and she is).

Mrs. Ivy had to watch and remind them for a few days before it became habit, but in real life, we never expect everyone to get it right the very first time. Her class became a model for others, and she was never again disgusted at the eating habits of her students. The real beauty is that she managed to teach table etiquette during math class. She made the lesson real, and therefore the students engaged in it and learned—two lessons at once! This is a terrific example of real-life teaching!

Example 2

Mr. Jaxon is about to introduce a new novel to his ninth graders. Thus far, he has observed that his students are reluctant readers. After looking at the individual cumulative records of his students, he sees a common thread: They are all reading below grade level.

Reasoning tells him that students who are poor readers and avoid reading at all costs will never improve their reading skills. Therefore, it is his job to get them to *want to read* and improve their reading skills in the process.

Mr. Jaxon selects a high-interest novel. It is one that he knows the students will enjoy, but only if he can get them to read it in the first place! The novel deals specifically with the death of the main character's mother and the aftermath of her death.

Mr. Jaxon begins by telling the students a personal story about how he lost his mother when he was 15 years old. He tells them about the effects that her death had on him, not only at the time but until this day. He encourages and welcomes input from his students, and a lengthy sharing session commences. Some students share that they have either lost a parent or know someone who has.

Mr. Jaxon tells them a little bit about Tommy, the main character in the story that they are about to read. "Judging from this discussion, you all are going to love the story we are about to read. It's about a 14-year-old boy whose mother is killed in a car accident. His mother is killed early in the story, but you'll learn more about her through Tommy's flashbacks throughout the story. Can anyone remember what a 'flashback' is?" Several students raise their hands. "It's when you reflect upon something that already happened," answers one student. "You've got it," says Mr. Jaxon. "And you won't believe some of the things that Tommy remembers as the story progresses! When I first read this book, I just couldn't put it down. It was that good!"

Mr. Jaxon has their attention. He has hooked them, and he doesn't want to lose their engagement by assigning several chapters to read. Experience has taught him that doing so would be a good way to lose their engagement. So, he asks them to sit back, relax, and open their novels to page one. He reads the first paragraph—a very powerful one—and then stops. He leads the students in a discussion about what has happened in the story and what they think might happen. He notices that the unfamiliar word *culmination* is used in the story, and he encourages them to use context to arrive at its meaning, and they do so with his guidance.

Once Mr. Jaxon is certain that all of the students understand what they have read and that all of them are still engaged, he continues reading. He teaches the entire first chapter in the same way: through discussion, prediction, vocabulary usage, and comparisons to other texts and to the students' own lives. At the end of the first chapter, he allows them to answer some questions, but he is certain they will be able to do so because he has led them in the right direction. Plus, once the students have finished answering the questions, the questions and answers are dissected during a lengthy discussion.

Mr. Jaxon found innovative ways of "attacking" the remainder of the novel. He used teacher read-alouds, student oral readings, silent reading, partner reading, and cooperative groupings. He devised a number of ways to keep them engaged. The novel took what some might consider a long time to complete, yet the end result was worth the time and effort. Some might call his methods "fanfare" or a waste of time. Mr. Jaxon, however, viewed them as successful teaching and learning experiences. By using these real-life teaching strategies, he managed to engage the students in the book. The students understood the story line. Mr. Jaxon enjoyed teaching, and the students enjoyed learning. What more is there?

Example 3

Ms. Dupre is a high school biology teacher who wants her students to *want* to be in involved in her biology lessons. In the upcoming unit, she must teach students about the growth rate of a centipede. Ms. Dupre orders several bags of centipedes (yes, real, live ones). They arrive on the afternoon before she is to begin the unit with her students. She takes one look at them and knows exactly how she will introduce the lesson so as to involve and engage her students.

Have you ever heard of the "Wow factor"? Well, it definitely applies here. When the students enter the classroom the following day, their desk arrangement has been changed. Ms. Dupre has arranged the desks around a large lab table, which is now in clear view of all of the students. Ms. Dupre gingerly walks toward the table with the bag in her hands. (The students cannot see what is in the bag, but its contents are about to be revealed!) Ms. Dupre allows the students to get settled (changing the desk arrangement at any time is always cause for a minor uproar) and then proceeds with the "revelation." She pours a huge bag of the creepy little creatures right onto the lab table! (In case you didn't already know what the "Wow factor" is…this is it!) Students oohed and aahed. Some pretended not to be bothered, and others raced from their desks.

A centipede may be an ugly, bloodcurdling little creature, but it is perfectly harmless. (Try telling that to the young lady who is hanging from the light fixture!) Ms. Dupre decides to prove this to the students by handling one of the creatures. This is a biology class, and the students are accustomed to handling creatures of all sorts, so they settle down quickly. The result, however, is that she has their attention. They are listening when she tells them how quickly these creatures can grow. In fact, while she is talking about the rapid monthly growth rate of the centipede, she encourages the students to write a mathematical equation to figure out how large a small centipede will be in one month, two months, etc.

The lesson progressed in much the same way, but the bottom line was that instead of just giving the students notes, showing a film, or lecturing about the growth rate of a centipede, she made it real to them. And the lesson doesn't get any more real than a bag full of live centipedes released from captivity just inches in front of the students' faces!

What Doesn't Work

 ### Example 1

Today is "vocabulary day" in Ms. Johnson's class. The students know exactly what to do on vocabulary day because they are well practiced. They have had a vocabulary day every Monday for the entire first semester of school. The lesson goes something like this:

- ◆ The bell rings.
- ◆ The students get out their notebooks and dictionaries.
- ◆ The teacher flips the switch on the overhead projector, displaying a list of words.
- ◆ The students look up the words in the dictionary and copy the definitions into their notebooks.
- ◆ Many students are off task during the lesson.
- ◆ Some students fall asleep during the lesson.
- ◆ Some students are creative and devise their own lessons.
- ◆ Some of these creative students are referred to the office.
- ◆ The bell rings and the students exit the room.

The students are not engaged because they are not learning. They are not interested because these unfamiliar words are not yet real to them. They are unable to make a connection between the words themselves and the words used in context because they have never seen them in context!

They know to expect at least 20 to 25 words per week. The words are always taken from the upcoming story in the textbook...the story that will be read on Tuesday, after they have completed the vocabulary assignment. They know that if they do not complete the vocabulary in class, the remainder can be completed as homework. The students copy words and definitions for one hour per week, every Monday, week in and week out. Friday is the test—every Friday.

Can you guess what the assignment is on Tuesday?

- The bell rings.
- The students get out their textbooks.
- The teacher assigns a particular story to be read silently.
- The students (some of them) read the story.
- The students (some of them) answer the questions at the end of the story.
- Many students are off task during the lesson.
- Some students fall asleep during the lesson.
- Some students are creative and devise their own lessons.
- Some of these creative students are referred to the office.
- The bell rings and the students exit the room.

I won't bore you with any more of the week's lessons, but suffice it to say that effective teaching did not take place. Obviously, real-life teaching was nonexistent. Unfortunately, we've all had "vocabulary" days and "read the story and answer the questions" days. We know that real-life teaching cannot take place in these types of lessons because they are devoid of real-life connections.

Dictionaries and textbooks are great teaching tools, but the teacher must bring them to life!

Example 2

Mr. Mathews is a social studies teacher who can tell you the name of every major city, state, capital, country, region, river, and lake in the world. He knows the name of every historical figure from Christopher Columbus to Martin Luther King, Jr. He knows the years of birth, death, and every monumental happening in their entire lives. Give him a name, and he'll render a quote.

Unfortunately, Mr. Mathews does not understand the concept of real-life teaching. He does not understand that every student has not had the same life experiences that he has had. Mr. Mathews's teaching strategies, which include lecturing, note taking, and testing, have led to very poor test scores.

A typical day in Mr. Mathews's classroom looks something like this:

- The students enter the classroom and take out their notebooks.
- Mr. Mathews begins his monotonous lecture.
- The students feverishly take notes.

- Mr. Mathews continues his monotonous lecture.
- The students feverishly take notes.
- Mr. Mathews completes his monotonous lecture.
- The bell rings and the students exit the room.

Because Mr. Mathews's students are struggling to keep up with the note-taking procedure, the information that the teacher is spewing is completely bypassing the minds of the students and landing directly in their notebooks!

Students in Mr. Mathews's class realize that to earn an A on Friday's test, they must be able to copy quickly and memorize aptly. Those who do not take sufficient notes don't have a chance of scoring well on the test because all of the "learning" comes from the note taking. Friday's test is really proof of two things: note-taking skills and memorization skills.

Unfortunately, Friday's test does not provide evidence that the students have learned much about history. Further proof could be gained if Mr. Mathews were to "pop" that same test (on the ones who do score A grades) a few weeks later. Something tells me that those A grades would be "history"!

Summary

 For something to be real to us, it must have happened to us or affected us in some way. We must be able to create some relationship with it for it to be authentic. If we can relate to a topic, we will willingly bring it into our consciousness as something that we can use in some way.

On the other hand, if we do not view something as important or valid in our lives today, we may reject it as immaterial. We're just not interested if we cannot make a connection.

Helping students make that connection is a difficult task, at best. Without that connection, however, teaching occurs in a vacuum. Sometimes, the teacher is alone inside the vacuum while the students are floating around somewhere else in space!

None of us wants to teach to four walls, yet we see it happening in far too many of our classrooms. Teachers have the power to change that. The information may exist in a textbook, workbook, or computer program, but the teacher is the source that brings it all to life. Don't exist in a lifeless classroom. Instead, make it real, and they will come!

I am me, I am not you
I can hear you when you speak
I listen, but I do not understand
If I cannot understand today, and could not understand yesterday
I will not understand tomorrow
You can say it again, and again, over and over
But it means nothing
I do not disrespect you; I simply do not understand you.

When you show me, the picture becomes clearer
Like a light illuminating a darkened room
Where before I was scared and lost
The picture is familiar, and I feel that I have been there
I am able to connect and would like to see more.

When you allow me to do it, I understand
It makes sense, so I embrace it
You assist me at first, but I am comfortable when set free
I will not quit, because now I am involved
I yearn to do more
Please allow me, and
I will show you that I can learn…

Elizabeth Breaux

Different Strokes: Accommodating All the Differences

We are all different. We are different in our appearance, in our dress, and in our likes and dislikes. We come from different backgrounds. We are of different religions and ethnic groups. None of us dispute these facts. Like it or not, everyone is not like us! That includes learning styles, learning preferences, and learning abilities. Yet if I, as a teacher, choose to teach students in only one way, using only one style and limited teaching strategies, I am excluding all of the students who are not exactly like me!

With this knowledge, we must recognize and buy in to the need to accommodate the many differences in learning styles by structuring our lessons so that instruction can be differentiated and meet the needs of all students. "But I have 26 students in my class," you say. "Am I to create a different lesson for each one?" Of course not! That would not be feasible in any setting. However, you can create an environment that blends different methods of instruction. You can vary your instructional strategies and activities so that you reach all students.

We must distance ourselves from the old one-size-fits-all theory. It is no truer in shoe and glove sizes than it is in lessons. (And I have *never* understood it in the clothing industry.) If we continue to accept this theory in the classroom setting, we are perpetuating the practice of teaching only the students who actually fit into that one-size-fits-all XXL t-shirt!

In every classroom, in every school, students function at different learning levels. Unfortunately, grade level and actual learning level are not always synonymous. Assuming that we are in agreement on this point, what would happen if we took a class of students at different learning levels and taught them all at the same level? What would happen, unfortunately, is that we would teach only the students at that level. Invariably, some would be bored because you would be talking down to them, and some would be lost because they had not yet arrived at that higher level.

In my experience, I have found that the use of cooperative grouping, workstations, and team teaching are excellent ways for one teacher to address the individual needs of students within one class setting. Keep in mind that when using cooperative grouping as a teaching strategy, you must be flexible (the makeup of groups should be continuously changing), you must be organized, and you must be an impeccable classroom manager! I hear it all the time, and frankly, I am more and more disgusted every time I do: "My kids are too bad to work in groups. I just give them enough work to keep them busy on their own." One teacher recently said to me, "My kids can't handle all of that fancy stuff." (My question to her would be this: "Is it really the *kids* who can't handle the fancy stuff?")

Teaching is not for the faint of heart—that's why we *chose* to teach. We knew that we were ready for the challenge. And it is challenging. None of us would dispute that. If you are a teacher who is unfamiliar or uncomfortable with the concept of differentiating instruction, or if you find it extremely challenging because you think that it's too much work or that the students can't handle it, the following tips for accommodating differences are sure to help. Please give them a try.

Tips for Accommodating Differences

- Be organized! (See Chapter 10)

- Become a great classroom manager. (See Chapters 4 and 5)

- Learn about your students. If you've been teaching the same class for a while, you already know them fairly well. If it's the beginning of the year, have them complete a learning styles inventory. There are some great ones out there.

- Ask your students. They'll be happy to share their likes and dislikes when it comes to teaching methods, class activities, learning environments, and study practices.

- Make a list of some of the teaching strategies that you use most frequently, and then add some that you have been reluctant to use. Focus on implementing many different ones. (A list of strategies follows.)

- Plan well for the lesson. Have all materials and activities in order and ready.

- If you are going to use a strategy that you have never used before, be ready to teach, practice, and implement the procedures for doing so.

- Be willing to create varied group assignments in which each student in the group is given a different task or assignment.

- If you are going to use stations in your room for the first time, be ready to teach, practice, and implement the procedures for doing so. Stations allow for materials to be presented to students in a variety of ways.

- If you are going to use peer assistance or peer tutoring for the first time, be ready to teach, practice, and implement the procedures for doing so.

- Prepare activities that are hands-on and activity based.

- Use rubrics for assessing students' work. (See Chapter 14)

- Make certain that you are actively involved at all times.

- Do some research on learning styles, multiple intelligences, and differentiated instruction. You'll get great information and ideas for implementing new strategies and techniques.

Sample Teaching Strategies
- Whole group
- Small group
- Modeling
- Question and answer (teacher directed)
- Question and answer (student directed)
- Open-ended questioning (develops critical-thinking skills)
- HOTS (higher-order thinking skills)
- Hands-on learning
- Guided reading
- Shared reading
- Integrated reading and writing
- Sustained reading and writing
- Technology
- Guided practice
- Peer tutoring
- Team teaching (teacher, teacher-assistant, adult tutor)
- Discussions
- Debate
- Problem-solving activities
- Critique
- Role playing
- Teaching with visual aids
- Brainstorming
- Graphic organizers
- Diagrams
- Study groups
- Books on tape
- Storytelling
- Lecturing

Use this list to evaluate what you are already doing and to guide your planning for future lessons. Remember that the intent is not only to vary instruction from day to day but also to vary instructional strategies within a class period or setting. In the "What Works" section, you'll see some excellent examples from classes that I have recently observed.

What Works

Example 1

I observed a first-year teacher who taught an eighth-grade regular education math class; however, this was an "inclusion" class that included several special education students. To accommodate these students, the special education teacher was part of a team that was teaching this class. In addition, this high at-risk school had used its tutoring funds to hire full-time tutors in the areas of math and English/language arts, so a third teacher also served on the team.

When I entered the room, it was immediately apparent that the teacher team had an excellent working relationship with the class and a solid plan in place. I saw several groups of students scattered throughout the room. Some were in groups of two or three. Three were at computers. One group of five or six students sat together in a far corner of the room. Everyone was talking, all at once, but the noise was structured and not distracting or overpowering in any way. All of the students were on task. The tutor was working with a group of five or six students. The two teachers were going from group to group and from individual to individual. I could not distinguish between the regular and the special education students. This was inclusion at its finest.

I noticed that the students at the computer were working on some sort of bar graph. (I didn't want to disturb them with my questioning, so that's all the information I know.) I noticed that one of the groups was working with manipulatives, and I was impressed by how all three were helping one another. The tutor was holding an ongoing question-and-answer and discussion session. She made use of a white board, and the students were displaying their answers in different colors. (I later learned from the teacher that they were working on mathematical equations in which colors had been assigned to specific parts.)

When I later spoke to the regular education teacher, I expressed my overwhelming certainty that students' needs were being met. Not only were their academic needs being met, but also their emotional needs were so obviously being filled. Furthermore, the need to include special education students in the "society of regular education" was being accommodated. I made a point of talking specifically to the special education teacher, who assured me that his students were doing better than they had in previous years, both academically and socially. He said that office referrals had dropped dramatically.

Note 1: I must add that this was not the first time that I had observed this new teacher, so I already knew that she was an excellent classroom manager. A setting such as the one I have just described will never be found in the classroom of a teacher who has not first become a good manager. It is a vital part of any lesson, and it can dictate a lesson's success or failure.

Note 2: I should also add that, in theory, this example might be viewed as a best-case scenario, considering that there were three adults in this classroom. In case you are tempted to think so, you should know that this was a very high at-risk school, one that had been labeled "academically unacceptable" by the state. The majority of the students there were performing below grade level.

Example 2

I walked into the gymnasium and expected to see students throwing balls into hoops. That's not what I saw at all. In fact, much to my surprise, I saw actual health and physical education taking place.

The classes consisted of a total of 62 seventh graders. The two teachers (who had decided to team teach on this particular day) had created stations around half the gym. (Another group of students was shooting hoops on the other side of the gym.) The team teachers had created 10 different stations. Each group consisted of about six students. All of the groups were moving from one station to the next at the sound of the teacher's whistle. Everything seemed extremely well managed, well organized, and highly effective. Let me describe for you exactly what was occurring:

- The students had been divided into groups, and each group had been assigned to a station.
- At the sound of the whistle, each group moved to the next station.

- The activity did not cease. The students moved for 30 minutes without stopping for a break. (I noticed that the students were carrying data cards on which they wrote information at each station.)
- The two teachers and about five students who had been designated "assistants" were moving from station to station, helping the groups.

Here's what I saw happening at the individual stations:

- Three heart-rate monitoring stations were interspersed throughout the stations. Students carried their own personal data cards with them from station to station. At the heart-rate monitoring stations, students took their own pulses (or had a teacher or assistant help them if necessary) and wrote down the information on their data cards. (I spoke to the two coaches and learned that during a previous health lesson, the students had learned how to monitor their exercising heart rate.)
- At the jump rope station, students picked up individual ropes and jumped for the allotted amount of time.
- At the log bend station, students picked up actual wooden logs, hoisted them onto their shoulders, and began to do deep knee bends. (I noticed that they were recording the number completed on their data sheets. Teachers and assistants were needed often at this station to help students maintain their form so as not to injure themselves.)
- At another station, the jogging station, students ran around the gym on a jogging course mapped out with red tape.
- Much assistance was given at the sit-up station, where some needed another person to help them.
- One assistant stayed at the long-jump station and recorded distances for the standing long jump. (I noticed the teachers going back and forth to this station often to help students improve their form and technique.)
- At the break station, students walked a line around the gym that was designated with green tape. (No assistance was ever needed at this station!)
- I noticed that the push-up station seemed to cause more grief than any of the other stations, but the teachers were always watching to make certain that the exercise was being performed properly and to lend assistance as needed.

And that's it! Because there were three heart-rate monitoring stations, the number of stations totaled 10. Students worked for about 30 minutes, but between the three heart-rate stations and the break station, they were not being overly taxed. It was obvious that some students (the more athletic ones) did not need as much assistance, but all were working at their own level. For example, one young man completed more than 100 sit-ups in the allotted three minutes, whereas another student completed just under 50. Both, however, were working at the required percentage of maximum heart rate, so they were working equally hard! (The heart-rate monitoring stations were created to ensure that all students worked at the required percentage of the maximum. Heart rate is an indicator of that.)

It was obvious that differences were being accommodated:

♦ The activities were varied.

♦ Assistance was given wherever needed by teachers and peers.

♦ Each student was working at his or her own levels (albeit on the same activities) while being challenged to improve.

I thought about and related this lesson to one that is often seen in the typical academic classroom. I imagined a classroom in which several stations have been set up. Students are working on different types of activities and using a variety of strategies. It is a math class, and the teacher has created the following stations:

♦ Station 1: Computer-generated tessellations

♦ Station 2: Creating tessellations using manipulatives

♦ Station 3: Exploring artwork: Finding the tessellations

♦ Station 4: Exploring the hallway for tessellations

♦ Station 5: Creating your own tessellations using construction paper

The teacher, of course, models expectations for each station and continuously monitors and assists once the station work begins.

What does the teacher inside you imagine for your students? Don't be afraid to be creative. Your students will be the benefactors of your hard work and creativity. Have fun!

What Doesn't Work

 Remember that the objective is to differentiate our instruction and activities so as to accommodate the many differences in our students. Remember that students need our assistance. Remember that if a student is failing, something is obviously not working!

Let's look at a list of some of the things that simply don't work.

+ Any activity in which everyone is doing the same thing in the same way all or most of the time
+ Lack of variety in teaching strategies
+ Lack of variety in activities
+ Lack of knowledge of the individual needs of the students
+ Busywork that requires no assistance from the teacher
+ Lack of individualized assessment practices

This list brings to mind a teacher from the last chapter—Ms. Johnson—whose weekly lesson plans all looked the same. If you remember, every Monday was "vocabulary day," when students used a dictionary and a notebook to define the week's list of words, and every Tuesday was "read the story silently day," when students read silently and answered questions. (Before you read the rest of the week, I must make it clear that I am not opposed to sustained silent reading. I am opposed to any teaching strategy that is used in isolation, over and over, and with no variation because it is a *prescription for limited or questionable success* for some and a *prescription for failure* for others!)

Let's look at a week in Ms. Johnson's class, and you decide whether the needs of all of her students are being met.

Monday:	Vocabulary
Tuesday:	Read the story silently
Wednesday:	Answer questions from the story
Thursday:	Complete worksheets from the story
Friday:	Testing

What do you think?

Summary

We must differentiate our instruction to afford students many different options for absorbing, digesting, assimilating, understanding, and using ideas and information. We must provide an environment in which students of different abilities can learn within the same class setting.

To accept or embrace the idea that in order to accommodate all differences, we must differentiate our instruction, we must first affirm in our own minds that students come to us with varied backgrounds of knowledge, interests, learning styles, and readiness. They are not all in the same place at the same time. If they were, teaching would not be only the easiest job in the world, it would also be the most boring!

Accommodating all students in one class setting is not an easy task or a slight undertaking. The weak of heart, mind, and will could never do it. That's why *we* are teachers. We want to teach, and we want our students to learn—all of them, not just the ones who are like us. We are committed to doing whatever it takes to achieve that goal.

When preparing an activity, assessment, or a task
"How am I to score this?" is the question I must ask
"And how will I let students know, precisely what's required
In order to receive the very score that they desire?"

I'm certain that they'd want to know exactly what to do
And just what I am looking for when I do my review
There should be no surprises, we all should understand
That I don't give them grades, I just record what they hand in!

I've never thought it fair to base a grade on my opinion
It seems to me that this would be abuse of my dominion
So I'll spell out precisely what it is that I expect
And they'll know that what they give me is exactly what they'll get!

Elizabeth Breaux

Using Rubrics for Assessment: When They Know, They Do

I started using rubrics for assessment several years into my teaching career. The term *rubric* was an unfamiliar one, and initially it received its fair share of ridicule for the name alone. I can remember when the term was first introduced to me. Now that I think about it, it was the strategy used to introduce the word that made that lesson memorable. I really do remember it vividly. I was at a teachers' workshop. The presenter gave a poster to each group. The word *rubric* was written in large print in the middle of the poster. We passed the poster around, and each of us was to write our own definition of the word onto the poster. Then, of course, someone from each group would present it (I've always hated that part). I remember how much fun we had writing our ridiculous "definitions" because we had little to draw on but our own imaginations, and they were running rampant!

None of us came up with the correct response, but it was a great introductory activity. It must have been because that was many years ago, and I still remember it well. (I can barely remember what happened yesterday!)

After that initial introduction, I was hooked! Rubrics became my most frequently used method of assessment. I remember when I started using them for writing assignments. I was teaching language arts to below-average middle school students, and their writing skills were basically nonexistent. However, through the guidance of rubrics, my students were writing in no time. After several weeks, they were actually writing well. My first rubric was very basic and looked something like this:

Paragraph Writing

_____ The paragraph is indented.
(1 point)

_____ The topic sentence is an attention grabber.
(1 point)

_____ Three or more details are used to support the topic.

(3 points)

_____ The paragraph is "wrapped up" with a good closing sentence.
(1 point)

_____ All sentences are complete.

(5 points)

_____ All sentences begin with a capital letter.

(5 points)

_____ All sentences end with correct punctuation.

(5 points)

Possible points that can be earned: 21

_____ Total points earned

_____ Your score

This rubric is very basic in its requirements because my students' writing abilities were at a very basic level. The writing that I had seen from them contained errors in all of the areas included in the rubric. When I brought these areas to their attention by placing them on the rubric and assuring the students that if they did everything that the rubric required, they would receive an A, they simply started doing them. It became a habit. I used rubrics to improve their writing skills throughout the year by adding requirements. I added things such as

- ◆ Compound sentences
- ◆ Subject–verb agreement
- ◆ Spelling
- ◆ Vocabulary words
- ◆ Figures of speech: simile, metaphor, hyperbole, alliteration, personification, onomatopoeia

I'll never forget the day we placed the students' first essays on the wall outside the room. The students had worked so diligently on them, and they were so proud. They were proud because of their success. They were proud because of their efforts. They were proud because they had total control over the grade that they earned; they had assumed that power and were running with it! A supervisor in the district happened to be in the building and noticed the essays on the hallway wall. She knocked on my classroom door, walked in, looked directly at the students and said to them, "This is some of the best writing I have seen from middle school students in a long time." The pride on their faces was palpable and indelible. It was one of those moments that will be with me forever. It was the icing on the cake for the students and the impetus they needed to build on their success.

Rubrics serve a variety of purposes:

- ◆ They set guidelines and parameters.
- ◆ They are precise and therefore remove the guesswork.
- ◆ They ensure that the teacher and students are on the same page regarding expectations.
- ◆ They make an assignment easy to score.
- ◆ They are a way to elicit as much or as little from the student as the teacher deems necessary.
- ◆ They force students to take total responsibility for the work that they do. (In other words, they can't blame the teacher for a poor score.)

Directions for some assignments can be ambiguous because teachers are often unclear in their expectations. Open-ended questions are often hard to score because our definition of a good answer and the students' definitions of a good answer are usually quite different. Rubrics take the ambiguity out of the mix.

The old way of testing students was unambiguous but also unchallenging. The old fill-in-the-blank, true/false, and "everybody gives the same answers" tests didn't require the use of a rubric because they didn't require the use of critical-thinking skills. Every question had a definitive answer. Every question was worth the same number of points. Thankfully, teachers have moved away from this type of testing because it does not assess students' abilities to use higher-order thinking skills. Subjective tests with open-ended questions require students to analyze and apply information. A well-constructed rubric will guide students toward the inclusion of the correct information in their answers.

Situation

 Test scores at this particular school have fallen steadily for three years in a row. If scores do not improve over the next two years, the school will fall into the lowest achievement category, according to state standards. The implications will be significant, and so the district has decided to use all of its resources to save this school from failure. The district hires an outside education consulting firm to do an in-depth study of the school, from the administration to the teachers, students, and custodial staff. Teachers who choose to stay at the school know that their classrooms will be scrutinized and their teaching evaluated on an ongoing basis. Sadly, some still believe that the old way works best and that the demise of the school lies solely in the hands of its students. Their refusal to change is apparent, and the underlying problems unfold in clear light.

What Works

 Mr. Albert is a social studies teacher, but he is not the typical teacher whom some of us remember. Early in his career, he used the old lecture, note-taking, memorization, and testing techniques, but he soon learned that his students were learning little and retaining even less. He became disillusioned by the reality that in failing to help his students make a connection with the subject matter, he was unable to make the much-needed student–teacher connection. He wanted his students to feel a natural love of history, as he did, but after many ineffective lessons, failing grades, and sleepless nights, he realized that *he* was the key ingredient. The students were not going to change. The school was not going to change. The parents were not going to change. And history was certainly not going to change in order to accommodate his teaching style! Mr. Albert wanted to be able to teach the subject he loved while at the same time teaching it in a manner that involved the students and gave them ownership of their grades.

In the past few years, Mr. Albert had been reluctant to change. However, he had noticed that the failure rate of his students had risen, and he was now determined to do whatever was necessary to rectify that. And then, Mr. Albert, a 22-year veteran of teaching, did the one thing that too many teachers are reluctant to do: He asked for help!

Mr. Albert attended every social studies workshop offered that summer. He brought valuable materials and innovative ideas back to the Social Studies Department. He shared what he had learned and invited others to do the same. And then he got to work, determined that this year would be different. It certainly was.

Members of the private consulting firm that had been hired to evaluate the school took immediate notice of Mr. Albert's classes. They were amazed at the level of interest and the fact that all of his students had passing grades. They were also amazed at the number of opportunities that students were given to earn grades. (The lack of opportunity had previously been one of Mr. Albert's most outstanding downfalls before this year—he used to teach and teach and teach and then gave one big test, which a large percentage of his students would fail.) The consultants noticed that Mr. Albert taught only in small increments, paying particular attention to the lives of historical figures and how they related to the lives of his students. The results of the compiled classroom observations showed that Mr. Albert

- Taught the material in small increments
- Related the lessons to the students' lives
- Encouraged discussions that required higher-order thinking
- Assessed students often and in a variety of ways using a subjective, higher-order format
- Used rubrics to assess daily quizzes, cooperative grouping assignments, projects, and tests

The following is a sample test item (and the accompanying rubric) from one of Mr. Albert's tests.

Describe the journey of Lewis and Clark.
Be sure to include (and attend to) the following in your description:

Preparations that they made (3 points)   ____

How they received funding for their journey (1 point)   ____

At least three obstacles that they faced along the way (3 points)   ____

At least three points of travel (3 points)   ____

Physical conditions that they faced (4 points)   ____

Your thoughts on ways they could have planned better (3 points)   ____

Neatness of description (3 points)   ____

Conventions of writing: indention, punctuation, complete sentences, capitalization (4 points)   ____

Possible points: 24

Points earned: ____

Your score: ____

Mr. Albert also changed his tactic of giving only cumulative tests every couple of weeks. Instead, he gave mini-assessments on an ongoing basis. (The foregoing sample question is the kind that he began to give in isolation, just to "spot check" from day to day.) He soon realized that by doing this, students were being given many opportunities to earn grades, their scores were better, and their overall success rate was higher. These small successes motivated the students to want to do even better, and the ball just kept rolling! It became crystal clear to Mr. Albert that in the old days, when he had tested only bimonthly, he had not given himself the opportunity (which he now had through these incremental assessments) to see exactly which students were absorbing the information and which were not. In the days before he used rubrics, his directions and expectations had been vague. His expectations had not met students' expectations of themselves. Now, through the use of rubrics, that, too, was crystal clear!

Mr. Albert was hooked! In addition to daily and cumulative written assessments, he began using rubrics for cooperative grouping activities and projects. The students in his classes got a taste of success, and once that happened, their taste buds yearned for more. The successful teacher that had lurked inside Mr. Albert for years now emerged. He chose to allow that to happen by opening his mind to change. He took responsibility for that change away from the students and assumed it himself. The results were astounding.

What Doesn't Work

 Directly across the hallway from Mr. Albert was the classroom of Mrs. Hanson. Suffice it to say that unlike Mr. Albert, Mrs. Hanson had not yet "arrived." Like Mr. Albert, the test scores in Mrs. Hanson's classes showed a marked decline over the past few years, but Mrs. Hanson was not ready to assume much responsibility for that. She simply continued to blame student and parent apathy for the decline while failing to acknowledge that she had the power to make a difference. (If you remember, Mr. Albert found a way to extinguish apathy: He simply showed his students they could succeed, and the apathy subsided as a result.)

Further review and countless observations supported what the administration already suspected:

- ◆ Mrs. Hanson often lectured while the students took notes.
- ◆ Mrs. Hanson used no alternative assessments. She stuck to the old "tried-and-true" cumulative tests.
- ◆ Class discussions were minimal and included few opportunities to improve critical-thinking skills.
- ◆ The majority of test items were objective.
- ◆ Rubrics were not used.
- ◆ Test scores were very poor and very few.
- ◆ Students did not have many opportunities to earn points and feel successful.
- ◆ Students had become accustomed to failure in Mrs. Hanson's class. Self-expectations were low.

When questioned, Mrs. Hanson blamed her students' poor performance on student apathy and lack of parental involvement. Mrs. Hanson's students did poorly again that year, to no one's surprise. The old definition of *insanity* comes to mind: *doing the same thing over and over again and expecting a different outcome!*

Summary

Change is difficult, but there is usually a good reason for it. Unfortunately, we sometimes lose the forest for the trees—especially those of us who have been in the forest for many years!

The old fill-in-the-blank, true/false, "everybody gives the same answers" tests didn't require the use of rubrics because they didn't require the use of critical-thinking skills. Every question had a definitive answer, stopping short of engaging the students in analytical thought. Thankfully, teachers have moved away from this type of testing because it does not assess students' abilities to use higher-order thinking skills. Subjective tests with open-ended questions require students to analyze and apply information. A well-constructed rubric will guide students toward the inclusion of the correct information in their answers.

If you haven't already done so, please don't be reluctant to try using rubrics as an assessment tool. Your students will thank you. Their parents will thank you. The administration will thank you. And that consulting firm will finally leave you alone so that you can get back to teaching! Real teaching…and real learning. Success for everyone. It's addicting. Try it, and you'll be hooked!

Summary of Part II

Teaching students—really *teaching* them—is no easy undertaking. It requires hard work, dedication, and a willingness to change. The students of a good teacher leave the classroom every day with knowledge that they did not previously possess.

Good teachers know that they must view each student as an individual with a different background, different requirements, and different abilities. Good teachers know that students cannot learn material they are not connected to. Good teachers know that they alone can be the key.

Those of us who have been there know that it gets better every year because *we get better every year!* We can truly become master teachers, as long as we are willing to acknowledge what doesn't work and change it.

Let's take a quick look at what the endeavor to teach students entails:

- I must be *well organized* in order to make efficient use of precious time.

- I must differentiate between *effective instruction* and teaching practices that are not effective.

- I must use *real-life teaching strategies* if I intend to bring the material to life for my students.

- I must recognize that *different strokes* are necessary if I am to accommodate all of the individual differences in my classroom.

- I must learn to embrace alternative types of assessment and incorporate *rubrics* as a powerful assessment tool.

You must believe in yourself and the awesome power that you have to make a difference in your classroom each day. You have the power, the tools, and the skills necessary to effectively teach all of your students. Acknowledge what works and make it even better. Acknowledge what doesn't and then make the necessary changes. So much of a student's success lies in the choices of his or her teachers. Make your students successful...you have the power!

Final note: I feel it necessary to add that in teaching, as in life, there are exceptions to every rule. There will be times when you will be faced with challenges that require outside intervention. Please do not be afraid to ask for help from school counselors, administrators, school psychologists, social services, and child welfare workers.

I Am a Teacher

I am a teacher, nothing more
From mind, to heart, to soul, to core
I've never earned some grand award
No fancy plaques adorn my wall
My way, few accolades have come
About me stories written, none
And history will but little space
Reserve for me to write my place
But I have seen a young man cry
I've watched a teardrop fill his eye
And looked into a prideful face
No dream begotten can replace
So sorrows and regrets are few
Of paths not taken, roads eschewed
Or chances lost and swept ashore
I am a teacher, nothing more…

Elizabeth Breaux

Conclusion

Once again, I am awed and humbled by the unbelievable duty that I have been put here to perform. I know that I must never take that responsibility lightly. I know that I have the power to make a difference and that I ultimately make the choices. I pray that I will always choose wisely and that students' needs will drive all of my decisions. The children—it truly is all about the children. For without "Puppies and People," I would not have truly lived…

If you'd like information about inviting Elizabeth Breaux to speak to your faculty or group, please contact her at lizooofarms@cox.net or call 337-857-1806 or 337-654-0040.